MW00774062

African Philosophy

Bloomsbury Introductions to World Philosophies

Series Editor
Monika Kirloskar-Steinbach

Assistant Series Editor
Leah Kalmanson

Regional Editors
Nader El-Bizri, James Madaio, Sarah A. Mattice, Takeshi Morisato,
Pascah Mungwini, Omar Rivera and Georgina Stewart

Bloomsbury Introductions to World Philosophies delivers primers
reflecting exciting new developments in the trajectory of world
philosophies. Instead of privileging a single philosophical approach as
the basis of comparison, the series provides a platform for diverse
philosophical perspectives to accommodate the different dimensions
of cross-cultural philosophizing. While introducing thinkers, texts and
themes emanating from different world philosophies, each book, in an
imaginative and path-breaking way, makes clear how it departs from a
conventional treatment of the subject matter.

Titles in the Series
A Practical Guide to World Philosophies,
Monika Kirloskar-Steinbach and Leah Kalmanson
Daya Krishna and Twentieth-Century Indian Philosophy,
Daniel Raveh
Māori Philosophy, Georgina Tuari Stewart
Philosophy of Science and The Kyoto School, Dean Anthony Brink
Tanabe Hajime and the Kyoto School, Takeshi Morisato
African Philosophy, by Pascah Mungwini

African Philosophy

Emancipation and Practice

Pascah Mungwini

BLOOMSBURY ACADEMIC
LONDON • NEW YORK • OXFORD • NEW DELHI • SYDNEY

BLOOMSBURY ACADEMIC
Bloomsbury Publishing Plc
50 Bedford Square, London, WC1B 3DP, UK
1385 Broadway, New York, NY 10018, USA
29 Earlsfort Terrace, Dublin 2, Ireland

BLOOMSBURY, BLOOMSBURY ACADEMIC and the Diana logo are
trademarks of Bloomsbury Publishing Plc

First published in Great Britain 2022

Copyright © Pascah Mungwini, 2022

Pascah Mungwini has asserted his right under the Copyright, Designs and
Patents Act, 1988, to be identified as Author of this work.

For legal purposes the Acknowledgments on p. vi constitute an extension
of this copyright page.

Cover design by Louise Dugdale
Cover image: Nobi_Prizue/Getty Images

All rights reserved. No part of this publication may be reproduced or
transmitted in any form or by any means, electronic or mechanical,
including photocopying, recording, or any information storage or retrieval
system, without prior permission in writing from the publishers.

Bloomsbury Publishing Plc does not have any control over, or responsibility
for, any third-party websites referred to or in this book. All internet addresses
given in this book were correct at the time of going to press. The author and
publisher regret any inconvenience caused if addresses have changed or sites
have ceased to exist, but can accept no responsibility for any such changes.

A catalogue record for this book is available from the British Library.

A catalog record for this book is available from the Library of Congress.

ISBN: HB: 978-1-3501-9649-0
       PB: 978-1-3501-9650-6
       ePDF: 978-1-3501-9652-0
       eBook: 978-1-3501-9651-3

Series: Bloomsbury Introductions to World Philosophies

Typeset by RefineCatch Ltd, Bungay, Suffolk NR35 1EF
Printed and bound in Great Britain

To find out more about our authors and books, visit www.bloomsbury.com
and sign up for our newsletters.

Contents

Acknowledgments

The idea of this book is a culmination of several factors including the desire to contribute philosophical literature that speaks to the priority questions of Africa and in the furtherance of world philosophies.

Some extracts from two of my published articles, "The critique of ethnophilosophy in the mapping and trajectory of African philosophy," *Filosofia Theoretica: Journal of African, Culture, and Religion,* 8 (3), 2019: 1–20 and "The question of recentring Africa: Thoughts and issues from the global South," *South African Journal of Philosophy,* 35 (4), 2016: 523–36, appear in Chapters one and four respectively, although these have been extensively reworked both in terms of thrust and argument. I would like to thank the editors of the two journals for permission to include them.

I also wish to thank Bloomsbury Publishers and the Series editors, in particular Monika Kirloskar-Steinbach who, since our chance encounter at the 2018 World Congress of Philosophy and in a number of subsequent philosophical discussions, provided further reason for me to embark on this project.

I am of course indebted to many colleagues with whom I have shared insights formally and informally in various philosophical discussions: Some of their thoughts referenced in this work have been inspirational, as has our very own philosopher elder in the department of Philosophy [University of South Africa], Prof. M. B. Ramose.

Lastly, I wish to thank my family, and in particular my wife and son, for their unwavering support.

Introduction: The Emancipative Mission

Contemporary discourse on African philosophy is closely tied to the historical adversities of the past, which account not only for its emergence but also for its distinctive tone, character, and mandate. This history, which is itself a bane, was paradoxically reconstituted into a creative force and a prelude to the struggle for liberation. Today the great conversation among the world's philosophical traditions—and one inconceivable not so long ago—is inching closer to being the new reality, although admittedly there remain recalcitrant remnants of philosophy's own equivalent of the Security Council keen to preside over the philosophical with inflexible orthodoxy. It may be too early to celebrate their waning grip on the enterprise but it is not inopportune to acknowledge the emerging reality of world philosophies that has been years in the making. Perhaps there is no better way to remind ourselves of this history, and how we as African philosophers got to be in that unenviable position, than to recall this submission by Edelglass and Garfield (2011: 4): "We live today in the aftermath of a long period of colonialism. One effect of colonialism has been to reinforce prejudices regarding the intellectual or cultural superiority of certain nations over others; another has been to impoverish and to disempower those who have been both colonized and disparaged. This is a serious, pervasive moral wrong." Put differently, we are confronted with the brutal legacy of a world still seething from all kinds of inequities which revolved primarily around the pernicious denial of the humanity of others. The history of African philosophy as an academic enterprise is thus to be understood against this unconscionable travesty. What we articulate in the remainder of this work should therefore be seen as part of an ongoing dialogue with this history. It is within this context that we focus attention on what can be described as the emancipative thrust in the practice of African philosophy and the imperative history places on the African philosopher, including what it means to philosophize in an unjust world. Given these historical circumstances surrounding its inception as an intellectual practice, African philosophy has been regarded as "the bearer of a mission"[1]—a mission that has been defined in a variety of ways and which continues to be articulated. The story of African philosophy can perhaps be summarized by the following two words: liberation and self-(re)discovery—broadly conceived. As it continues to unfold, philosophy in Africa has sought to establish itself as both a counter-hegemonic and reconstructive discourse, responding to the challenges history has imposed on it on one hand and, on the other, working to establish its own identity and priority questions in response to the specificities of the continent and the needs of its peoples, but of course, cognizant of the wider philosophical discourse unfolding in other similarly placed parts of the world. It can indeed be argued that from their different approaches and vantage points, African philosophers have tried their best to advance philosophy, theoretically and practically[2] as an enterprise defined by explicit commitments to questions of identity, liberation, and justice. In this growing history of African philosophy, the emancipative mission is a constant feature in a number of works, but of course, its expression varies with the different authors and depending on their preferred entry point into the discourse on African philosophy. For illustrative purposes, we shall provide very brief reviews of four authors to highlight how the emancipative mission is expressed, or rather expresses itself, through their work even as they address questions of philosophy from different angles. In this quartet of carefully selected eminent thinkers, we shall not concern ourselves with the differences or disagreements that separate them, but instead we shall focus on what we see as common concerns that they have pursued from their different perspectives on philosophy. Of course, we will occasionally comment on some of the differences in subsequent chapters as part of the productive friction which not only keeps the dialectic alive, but the philosophical enterprise itself going. And as it continues to grow and to attract more practitioners, African philosophy has begun to come to terms with its own increasing internal diversity, communities of discourse and equally adept globally engaged sub-communities. We begin our reflections with Masolo's *African Philosophy in Search of Identity*, a book described by Hallen (2002: 108) as "the first truly comprehensive and detailed history of African philosophy" and that, we presume, is because it has been able to trace the story of African philosophy without falling victim to the broad restrictive divisions of Francophone and Anglophone Africa. After presenting a thoroughgoing analysis of the history of African philosophy and as part of what constitutes his concluding remarks to the book Masolo (1994: 251) declared:

> There is no single philosophical tradition that was tailor-made and produced like an industrial product. There is no justifiable reason, therefore, why one individual or group should try to tailor-make African philosophy by prescribing what ought to be its content, method of reasoning, and standards of truth. Like other philosophical systems and traditions, African philosophy must also be born out of its own peculiar cultural circumstances combined with a living and constructive zeal amongst individual African intellectuals to understand and explain the world around them.

There is no prize for guessing what prompts this submission which is in itself a statement of conviction and an injunction against the imposition of methodological fetters and rigid orthodoxies on the philosophical practice. It is a salient reminder of that which is at stake—the freedom to define, to reimagine, and to express. Taken in that regard, the submission is of primary significance to all those engaged in the discourse and production of African philosophy. As Gordon (2019: 16) has recently made clear, "constraints on philosophy, . . . could take many forms, some of which are also paradoxical. . . . Other such concerns abound where philosophy is held subordinate to various ways of understanding what the pursuit or love of proverbial wisdom may be." It is apparent from the above that what Masolo envisions for African philosophy is a practice which should never be held subordinate to a specific conceptualization of the enterprise. After all, as Gordon (2019: 16) asks rhetorically, "What could a celebration of thinking and reasoning be if doing so were shackled?" There is therefore a clear desire to see African philosophy establish itself on its own terms and African philosophers have a significant role to play in that regard. They have to strive as much as possible to render African philosophy an African discourse. The force with which these points are expressed leaves no doubt whatsoever that there is a distinct mission at hand: that is, to establish African philosophy on the basis of its own historical circumstances as a tradition of philosophy alongside other philosophical traditions in the world. Inherent in the submission is the need to reclaim independence of thought and to inject into African philosophy the dynamism it deserves in the manner it has to unfold going forward. How to make African philosophy an African discourse is what should constitute the significant point of departure in this undertaking and it underlines a crucial aspect of the emancipative drive. It is noteworthy that even today there are still ongoing attempts to reimagine the philosophical enterprise and to recapture its richness and diversity in terms of both insight and expression. Being an emancipative practice, philosophy in Africa must guard against a particular form of intellectual servitude traceable to the inordinate influence of foreign structures and conceptual models on our thinking. No particular understanding of philosophy should be considered sacrosanct and therefore adopted as an article of faith. Ultimately, in refusing to be subordinated to a particular understanding of the enterprise, African philosophy will not only serve as an instrument of emancipation and a means with which to reassert the plural character of human thinking, but it will also enable it to showcase its own identity and its internal pluralism in the way various practitioners approach the discipline.

The next book that we will look at is Hountondji's *African Philosophy: Myth and Reality*, a book that is as popular as it is controversial, but which has done a great deal in placing African philosophy on the world map. Masolo (2000: 152) describes the author as "not only one of the most prolific African philosophers, but also one of the best and most widely read, and perhaps one of the most controversial." Of course, many would attest to the fact that since its publication, the book has become the "the bible of anti-ethnophilosophers" (Mudimbe 1988: 158), sponsoring in some of its strongest adherents an attitude of inquisitional intolerance akin to religious fundamentalism—but of course, that is not our main concern at this point. It is crucial though to indicate at the outset as Wiredu (2004: 4) clearly points out, that "in this [ethnophilosophy] controversy, Hountondji's dialectical resilience has been much on display. But he has not been averse to revision." There was a wrong that Hountondji saw as being perpetrated and which he regarded as in need of urgent attention. True African philosophy must dispense with that malady and in so doing set itself on the correct path to constituting itself as a proper philosophy. His book was in this regard a "firm stand against intellectual self-imprisonment and unanimism, [and an] insistence on the right to the universal, and its assertion in all cultures, based on their own preoccupations and concerns, [including] a vocation to invent not only locally viable solutions but also concepts whose validity transcends regional boundaries" (Hountondji 1996: vii). There is definitely nothing that should stand in the way of setting demands for African philosophy that are invariably the defining characteristic of other established philosophical traditions. As is made clear in the preface, "questioning ethnophilosophy [was] therefore a first step on the long road toward self-recovery and self-confidence" (Ibid: xxiv). From the foregoing there is an unmistakable mission for philosophy in Africa that can be discerned from his submissions. It would seem there is an unmistakable commitment and mandate for philosophy in Africa: It should assist in setting Africa on the path to intellectual freedom, and to do that it should avoid all pitfalls that may result in perpetual intellectual subordination and self-imprisonment. As he makes clear in the preface, "one definitely cannot overlook the demand that philosophy should, directly or indirectly, enable its practitioners to understand better the issues at stake on the political, economic, and social battlefields, and thereby contribute to changing the world" (Ibid.: xiii). Reading from the manner in which Hountondji protests against intellectual self-imprisonment, his work speaks to the emancipative mission in Africa. This is a position that is shared by many in Africa and it cuts across the disciplinary divides.

The third work that we will consider is Ramose's *African Philosophy through Ubuntu* (1999), a book whose title is as instructive as it is thought provoking. There is every reason to believe that by choosing to have it expressly stated in the title, Ubuntu holds the key to what the author perhaps perceives as not simply the foundation but the inspiration that should drive the practice of African philosophy. In his review of the book, Kimmerle (n.d) describes it as offering a new approach to African philosophy, proceeding as it does from the basis of Ubuntu. The book opens with the following curious statement: "Self-defence is a natural, perhaps even an instinctive reaction of all living organisms confronted with imminent injury" (Ramose 1999: ii). It is not very difficult to locate the thinking behind this statement. Familiarity with not only the history, but also the role that Western philosophy has played in providing the pretext and logical grounds for the oppression and subordination of the indigenous peoples around the world will shed light into the reasoning behind that opening statement. Philosophy in Africa has a crucial role to play in defence of the indigenous peoples against all kinds of iniquities traceable to the unjust occupation of the continent. With this single statement, the tone of the book is set, and in those few words its mission—the authentic liberation of Africa—is laid out. Of course, the meaning of that opening statement finds itself elaborated in subsequent sections:

> By virtue of this ever questionable right [of conquest], the victorious conqueror in the manifestly unjust wars of colonisation appropriated the sole, unilateral right to define and delimit the meaning of experience, knowledge and truth for the African and, of course, all the colonised and women the world over. On this basis, 'African philosophy' was simply inconceivable. It was held to be impossible as an experience since the African was by nature incapable of producing any philosophy at all.
>
> Ibid.: iii–iv

It still remains a mystery as to how, if not only for racist reasons, these so-called paragons of philosophy given the period in which they lived and the time they were writing, could not have heard of Anton Wilhelm Amo (1703–59), the brilliant "man from Ashantiland, who torn from his people at the age of [three]" (Hountondji 2002: 140), and brought to Germany, had distinguished himself as a philosopher and indeed, a true African intellectual in their very midst. Amo taught at the universities of Halle and Jena.[3] How could his presence, and indeed the presence of his own philosophical work among them, have eluded such "great" minds?[4] Back to the book, however, where within the introduction Ramose goes on to reveal what is at the heart of his philosophical project: "The assertion and the reaffirmation of the African's inalienable right to reason must serve as a means to an end, namely, the authentic liberation of Africa. Therefore, African philosophy contains an ineliminable liberative dimension" (Ibid.: iv). The grounding reason for the justification and defence of African philosophy, including its mode as an enterprise, is thus provided. As he clearly states, it is the prevailing African condition that makes this procedure necessary. In all this, the philosophical enterprise must not only be founded on and thus be firmly anchored to the principles of what it means to be human, but it must also within this vein proceed to address the injustices of history and ultimately re-inscribe the universality of our shared humanity in the creation of a just world. His emancipative mission for philosophy is very clear. And, in recognition of the enormity of this task, Ramose extends an invitation to other fellow researchers and scholars by declaring: "The major part of our intention is to open up discussion by suggesting areas of research. In this sense, the various chapters [of his book] may be seen as research proposals on African philosophy based on *ubuntu*" (Ibid.: iv). Anybody who has bothered to follow the growth and development of African philosophy over the years will agree that this invitation has been answered from across the world by some among the philosophers and theorists and it continues to be honoured through numerous articles, books and book chapters, including postgraduate dissertations inspired by the philosophy of Ubuntu and undertaken in many centers of learning around the world.

The last book which we wish to consider as part of this quartet of these brief reviews is Serequeberhan's *The Hermeneutics of African Philosophy* (1994), a book that "presents itself as a kind of manifesto about what the role of hermeneutical philosophy in Africa should be" (Hallen 2002: 64). What immediately catches the reader's attention before proceeding into the contents of the book itself is the dedication. The book is dedicated to "to all those who, sacrificing life and limb, have fought for and are still fighting for the complete emancipation of the African continent. It is in light of their endurance and sacrifice that our intellectual efforts have any sense or meaning." It is clear from the foregoing that the significance of our intellectual efforts as African philosophers derives from their being relevant to the liberation of our continent and its peoples. That struggle for liberation carries the same significance whether the aggressor or colonizing force is internal or external. African emancipation can be declared only when all of its peoples are free from being held hostage, whether by foreign powers or by other fellow Africans. It is critical that those engaged in African philosophy are willing to learn from the various African liberation movements and struggles in order to help reorient their own philosophical practice. Accordingly—and in the author's eyes—it is these historical, specific, concrete, and lived realities that should shape and give meaning to the direction that our philosophical practice in Africa must take. It follows therefore that, "the proper task of philosophy in Africa is that of systematically elaborating a radical hermeneutics of the contemporary African situation" (Serequeberhan 1994: 16). Philosophy must contribute towards the emancipation of Africa. Ultimately for Serequeberhan, it is important to remember that "philosophical discourse itself originates from and is organically linked to the concrete conditions-of-existence and the life-practices of the horizon within and out of which it is formulated. . . . this hermeneutical undertaking cannot but be a politically committed and historically specific critical self-reflection that stems from the negativity of our post-colonial present" (Ibid.: 17). It is clear that in advocating this context-oriented mode of philosophical practice, the goal is to deal with the problems of the unfinished and yet fundamental project of decolonization in Africa. This he makes clear by stating: "the hermeneutics of African philosophy must engage in situated reflections aimed at the pragmatic and practical aim of enhancing the lived actuality of post-colonial Africa" (Ibid.: 114). There can be little disagreement about the emancipative role that he sees for African philosophy. Our engagement in philosophy requires that we take a closer look at Africa's present condition and "reflect on the responsibilities at the level of ideas and thinking which this situation imposes on the contemporary discourse of African philosophy" (Serequeberhan 2015: 3). This is yet another way of elaborating on the philosophical mission in Africa, which as pointed out above is to contribute to the liberation of the continent socially, politically, economically, and otherwise.

What we have presented in these brief synopses is illustrative of the truth behind the statement that African philosophy is the "bearer of a mission"—a mission that has been variously articulated and one that continues to unfold in multiple and promising ways. Through these four carefully selected authors and although not in that order, we have travelled from the Horn of Africa, across to West Africa, then East Africa and finally down to the Southern tip of the continent. There is no other special reason for this selection over and above the need to demonstrate how the different philosophers picked from across the continent, articulate from their different perspectives, the emancipative mission of African philosophy. As samples of work on African philosophy, they all have their fair share of admirers and critics: such is the nature of philosophy, but that is not what concerns us at this point. The thread that draws these different works together (besides their obvious treatment of the same subject) is, to borrow the words of Irele (1996: 30), "a concern for the improvement of the quality of life on our continent." We should also at the same time hasten to state that what we have selected to highlight here is not in any way exhaustive of the ideas of these selected scholars. These are individuals to whose oeuvre one can never do justice in a brief characterization of this nature; suffice to say that with these brief reviews we have broadly painted the nature of the struggle and how some of Africa's leading philosophers have positioned themselves in this mission. In this book we add our voice to the emancipative mission in African philosophy within the context of the growing recognition and acceptance of world philosophies. The book is divided into five chapters.

Chapter One is an attempt to map the field of African philosophy with recourse to some of the significant moments and debates that have shaped its current form. The chapter draws on the analogy of map-making to analyze the development of African philosophy as a discipline. Almost every new entrant to the field of African philosophy as an academic study is introduced to "the critique of ethnophilosophy" as part of their initiation into the debate on the nature of African philosophy. Particular attention is paid to this famous critique, including an assessment of the effects it may have had on the outlook of African philosophy and its expression as an unfettered practice. Powerful as it was, the critique of ethnophilosophy had both beneficial as well as unintended negative consequences on the development of African philosophy. The former are well known and documented but the latter are less explored. In spite of all the laudable outcomes in the sense of alerting Africans to a lurking methodological snare, the vehemence of the critique and its iconoclastic polemic may have triggered a self-imprisoning hesitancy and fear to experiment with available options at a critical stage in the progressive fashioning of a discipline that was yet to establish its own credentials. Our attention in this chapter is on the latter. In this exposition it is always crucial to remember that it was through the efforts of the first crop of African philosophers that the field has grown to what it is today.

Chapter Two is a response to one of the serious problems threatening African philosophy, that is, the "excessive scruple or hesitation" to immerse oneself fully in the exploration of indigenous cultural resources for philosophical ideas and insights for fear of supposed ethnophilosophical contamination. The chapter brings into sharp focus the connection between history, culture, and philosophy. There is a sense in which these sources continue to suffer complete neglect and are thus underexplored in our philosophical ruminations. True liberation begins at the level of understanding ourselves, our own history, and intellectual traditions—it is about African self-apprehension. The chapter turns its attention on the internalities of Africa in the sense of raising critical questions about where we are with the process of self-(re)discovery and where this has remained problematic.

This is then followed by an attempt in Chapter Three to look beyond the boundaries of African philosophy and to examine the philosophical potential that lies hidden but can be made manifest through intercultural dialogue. The chapter sets itself out as a response to that all important question: What can be done in order to be true to both philosophy and to humanity? A response to this question which takes the history of philosophy into consideration and aspects of how philosophy has been and continues to be practiced in other parts of the world, culminates with proposals on how philosophy can be transformed into a critical creative encounter that is truly enriching within the context of an unremittingly homogenizing world.

In Chapter Four, we turn our attention to the problem of the unfinished project of decolonization on the epistemic front with specific focus on the question of recentering Africa. Recentering, as the name suggests, is an attempt to center Africa again—to "demarginalize Africa, and to place it firmly at the center of its own history in a world that is henceforth plural; a world whose unity cannot be the result of annexation, or some kind of hegemonic integration, but of periodic re-negotiation" (Hountondji 2002: 141). We frame our discussion of this issue within the broader counter-hegemonic struggles for epistemologies from the global South. In this quest to reaffirm African historicity and agency, emancipative struggles such the "Rhodes Must Fall" movement are analyzed, as are questions of the philosophical canon itself including the pursuit of "strategic particularism." The need for epistemic justice must translate into a concomitant struggle to accord voice to the African and with it the path to intellectual independence. To borrow the words of wa Thiong'o (1987: 87), for those of us in African philosophy, decolonization is in and of itself "the search for a liberating perspective within which to see ourselves clearly in relationship to ourselves and to other selves in the universe." It is a humanistic struggle and endeavor with roots that reach back to the liberation struggles of yesteryear, the promises of which are yet to be fully realized on many fronts.

And finally, Chapter Five pays attention to the promise of world philosophies as an emerging reality. It takes as its point of departure the position that philosophy progresses not simply by celebrating its successes, but by paying closer attention to some of its most serious mistakes and failures. The turn to world philosophies is illustrative of this crucial reminder. The different philosophies are analogized to different streams and rivers that traverse the different territories being shaped by their own local terrain but also at the same time reconfiguring it. This chapter places African philosophy in the context of world philosophies as a reaffirmation of the emancipative mission, and it does so with recourse to Ubuntu philosophy as an example of a tradition of thought and a philosophical approach that has now distinguished itself as a subfield in African philosophy with its own distinct orientation and set of priority questions. Grounded in an ontology of be-ing while drawing from African experiences, from the concrete, and the ethical, and armed with a clear understanding of the ontological oneness of humanity, Ubuntu emancipative philosophy lays out a philosophical practice which can become a veritable instrument of change worldwide not only in our relationships as human beings but with the entire environment. We conclude the chapter with a note on the need to honour the worldliness of philosophy by restoring to the practice its richness and diversity.

The Terrain of African Philosophy

Introduction

Over recent decades, African philosophers have recorded notable achievements in terms of advancing the discipline of philosophy theoretically and practically as an enterprise by which they sought "to affirm and assert their humanity through a vindication of their rationality" (Ramose 1999: 8). This testimony, however, does not seek to play down the challenges, disagreements, and controversies that have characterized the discipline since its inception. A brief look at the history of philosophy in general would reveal that philosophy is characterized by various challenges such as methodological and definitional controversies, including antagonistic opinions on how best to produce it. However, despite the existence of such contestations, competing positions, and disagreements on how best to proceed, philosophers have not stopped philosophizing and nor have they contemplated laying down their tools until such controversies have been resolved. In fact, if they had tried to do the latter, their tools would still be down. Philosophy has continued to flourish, to a large degree spurred on by these seemingly intractable disagreements and controversies. It is from these varied approaches and divergent opinions on how best to proceed—how to carry out the philosophical mandate—that different schools of philosophy were born. In fact, it's probably not too far off the mark to conclude that the beauty of philosophy lies in this variety; in these contestations over how best to represent or contemplate reality and experience. A closer look at the history of Western philosophy reveals a field characterized by a variety of streams of thought, with some among them almost irreconcilable. In that cacophony, if one may call it that, there are Kantians, Hegelians, Heideggerians; there are Kuhnians, Popperians, Wittgensteinians; there are followers of Foucault, Derrida, Ricoeur; there are neo-Aristotelians, neo-Thomists.... Most of these philosophies started as attempts to put an end to the battle of the schools. The attempts soon became schools themselves and joined the battle.... So, disconnection is the rule and harmony not just the exception- it simply does not exist.

Feyerabend 2011: 8–9

It would seem therefore, that even the most emphasized traditional divisions in Western philosophy—that is, of the Analytic versus the Continental schools of thought—is a much-simplified version of the multiplicity of views and divisions that have characterized Western philosophy as a tradition.

Given the historical evolution of academic philosophy in Africa and its connection to Western philosophy in more ways than one, the emergence of different schools—including controversies over the definition and nature of philosophy—seemed inevitable. In an effort to define both the form and content of the field called African philosophy, philosophers on the continent had to involve themselves in serious cartographic work of a special kind. In other words, they had to commit themselves to some form of boundary work in order not only to delineate the area that they thought would appropriately constitute the field called African philosophy, but to distinguish and protect it from disreputable works, charlatans, and impostors. Through this seemingly innocent but crucial academic exercise, the foundation of what we consider today as African philosophy was laid, with some of its foremost practitioners and their contributions canonized, and others conversely deprecated. In this chapter, we argue that the process of mapping the field called African philosophy may have been impacted by a self-imprisoning hesitancy and fear to experiment with available options in the progressive fashioning out of a discipline that was yet to establish its own identity. This chapter is divided into two broad sections. The first section draws on the analogy of map-making to analyse the development of African philosophy as a discipline. In the second section, particular attention is paid to the critique of ethnophilosophy, including an assessment of the potential effects it may have had on the growth and development of African philosophy. The idea is not to retrace the arguments that constitute the critique and their proponents, but to draw attention to a hidden side of this critique, to what one could call its unintended negative consequences. This is then followed by a brief conclusion.

Mapping the Terrain

In his book *Cultural Boundaries of Science*, Gieryn (1999) applies the geometrical metaphor of map-making—the drawing and redrawing of boundaries—to analyse contestations over epistemic authority and credibility involving science and other cognate disciplines. Just like science, the history of philosophy is characterized by similar struggles and disputes in which attempts were made to guarantee the integrity of the discipline and to protect its claim to credibility and epistemic authority against other infiltrators and pseudo-claimants to the title. In fact, it can be argued that "philosophers have given more attention to the mapping of philosophy when it comes to the jurisdiction of philosophy over some methods or content, or the assigning of methods or content to others" (Janz 2009: 29). Serious effort was taken to maintain clear boundaries between philosophy proper and other related disciplines such as religion, theology, history, poetry, and literature studies, among others. The point we wish to make is that in their history, different disciplines—not just philosophy—have involved themselves in extensive cartographic work. During this process of boundary-mapping—that is, demarcation, border-marking, inclusion and exclusion—disciplines seek not only to assert their identity but also to assert and claim unrivalled authority in particular fields of enquiry and of human and social experiences. Throughout their existence, disciplines have been locked in these relentless wars of continuity against threats to their integrity and survival. In this high-stakes game, there is therefore a permanent commitment to boundary work, a ceaseless policing of borders and a persistent epistemological vigilance, in order to contain and repel the always-imminent assaults of irrationality. Gieryn (1999: 23) describes this boundary-work as "strategic practical action," in that ideological and epistemological positions are adopted by scientists and scholars alike to justify their own position and to maintain it while at the same time discrediting opponents or holders of opposing views. From drawing boundaries to patrolling and protecting those frontiers, disciplines remain on high alert, repelling opponents, expanding their fortunes, and making alliances where necessary as they adapt to ensure they stay ahead and remain alive. This will probably remain so until that point disciplines cease to exist as autonomous and independent fields of inquiry.

In order to establish itself as a tradition of thought and practice, African philosophy had to contend with the politics of being a philosophy whose existence had been summarily denied by demonstrating not only the fallacies of such a position, but by also establishing its own credentials as a philosophy. This is an issue which preoccupied almost everyone among the first generation of African philosophers. In other words, African philosophy needed not only to reclaim its space against the Western philosophy that constituted the philosophy of the center, but to also define itself. It was time to spell out to itself what that tradition of thought which now claimed a stake on the philosophical field should look like. A dual task was thus awaiting, namely: reclaiming the historicity of African existence through a counter-critique of the myth of modernity and Eurocentrism as the dominant ideology; and establishing itself, its own set of credentials as a practice—a contending tradition of philosophy. While there was near unanimity on the first task, the second was more contentious, in particular, on the question of method and the definition of African philosophy. And true to its nature as a philosophy, this evolution was marked by internal contradictions and dispute as the practitioners sought not only to map out the contours of the discipline, but also to distinguish its credentials as a truly philosophical enterprise. At this local level, and as individuals, African philosophers had to commit themselves to some cartographic work in order not only to establish the jurisdiction of their discipline, but also to lay out its methodological and epistemological foundations as an enterprise. In a period spanning the publication of Tempels's *Bantu Philosophy* (1945) on the one hand and the debate that ensued coinciding with the publication of the famous book by Hountondji, *African Philosophy: Myth and Reality* on the other hand, and during the years immediately thereafter, a clear picture had begun to emerge in terms of the inspiration, the currents, and the concerns that defined the field of African philosophy. It was on the basis of this emerging picture that the late Kenyan philosopher Odera Oruka (1944–95) was able to assess the field and convince himself that there were in existence different schools, distinct trends and approaches that defined the discipline. He initially distinguished four approaches or schools, to which he later added two more to bring the total up to six. As summarized by Hallen (2002: 53):

> The four trends, schools, or approaches to African philosophy he [Oruka] identifies are ethnophilosophy (Tempels, Griaule, Mbiti, and, as this category was first delimited, Gyekye, Hallen, and Sodipo); philosophical sagacity (Oruka); nationalist-ideological philosophy, which included African social-political thinkers (Fanon, Nkrumah, Nyerere); and professional philosophy, which he associates with the orthodox Western academic tradition (Bodunrin, Hountondji, and, as this category was first delimited, Wiredu and, most interestingly, Oruka himself again). [Later Oruka added two more approaches]: the hermeneutic, to more specifically accommodate those who choose a linguistic approach (Wiredu, Gyekye, Hallen, and Sodipo) and the artistic or literary, to apply to African intellectual figures in the humanities who address themselves to themes basic to Africa's cultural identity (Okot p'Bitek, Ngugi wa Thiong'o, and Wole Soyinka).

The foregoing represents Oruka's pioneering attempt to map out the field of African philosophy. This process was meant to designate, to demarcate, isolate, and classify the different available works that constituted the literature on African philosophy. Through this Oruka not only identifies the different approaches and schools, but he also provides a summary of each of the approaches including an example of works that fitted into each of the categories. At this point, it is not difficult to see how, through these demarcations, Oruka begins a process of mapping the field and of creating delimitations that would have a lasting effect on the perspectives and patterns of intellectual practice in African philosophy for years to come. As Janz (2009) correctly points out, this initiative to map the space of African philosophy was simultaneously the move to proclaim its borders, gatekeepers, laws, and citizenry. It is apparent that in this process of mapping, "the borders between African and non-African thought, between forms of African thought, as well as the borders between traditional and modern thought" (Janz 2009: 16) would influence the process. Oruka's effort not only helped to lay out the difference in character among the approaches, but also it distinguished the supposedly philosophical dead ends and illusory paths from the promising routes for the development of the discipline going forward. Equally significant in this layout is the fact that right from the onset, the field and practice of African philosophy were characterized by a plurality of approaches just like in any other tradition of philosophy. Even the difficulty of having clear demarcations between the approaches becomes clear if one looks at the fact that some individuals and their works had to be reclassified on second look; interestingly, Oruka inserted himself in more than one category. While the idea here is not to debate whether or not Oruka was right with his classifications, it is significant to note that the divisions themselves implied that an inherent hierarchy of philosophicality existed among the approaches. We cannot ignore the fact that there is something pernicious in designating one of the schools "professional," which somehow implies that all the other five approaches (and the scholars whose works fall under the other schools) are not "professional" philosophers. Even the justification that such a designation was meant solely to emphasize the fact that this was the trend to which those who shared the orthodox Western orientation belong, does not suffice. It was probably for this reason that Oruka had to include himself in two categories since he was both a professional philosopher by training, but committed to sage philosophy. The classifications themselves may point to something more than simple differences in approach. And equally interesting is the initial inclusion of some of Africa's eminent philosophers under the enthnophilosophy trend, which is somehow revisited and then changed. The question is: What had changed? The content they published had not. Could there have been some form of prejudice against those immersing themselves fully into a domain of philosophy that required a serious study of African culture and its resources right from the start? Was such insider knowledge irrelevant to professional philosophy proper? These are questions that may arise as part of this speculative exercise which has invariably serious practical implications. One of the significant outcomes is that with this classification Oruka helped to make apparent not just the different schools, but also the implicit hierarchization through the choice of nomenclature. With the help of this schema, it is possible not only to understand the genesis but also the mechanisms through which exclusionary tendencies announced their arrival onto the field of African philosophy with significant consequences for both its future practice and outlook. It is to this and other issues that we now turn.

The Critique of Ethnophilosophy Revisited

"Fires, as forestry experts tell us, have a beneficial effect in the economy of nature: they clear the ground for new and more vigorous growth" (Serequeberhan 2015: 54). How does this opening statement relate to the topic of discussion in this section? We now turn our attention to the point we wish to make with the analogy. Notwithstanding other contending views concerning the efficacy of fire as a forest management tool, we use this analogy to draw attention to two important things in the history of African philosophy and its ascendency to the academic discipline that it is today. On the one hand, we employ the analogy to capture the role played by the first crop of academic African philosophers who, through their efforts, cleared the ground for African philosophy to take root. Credit must go to this first crop of philosophers, whose energy and devotion began the process of cultivating this largely virgin territory into a productive field. Their scholarly contributions and debates around the nature of African philosophy set the field ablaze. Some among them were literally "breathing fire" in their protest against what they perceived as serious injustices concerning the project and trajectory of African philosophy. In openly deploring what they saw as a continuation of the colonial project disguised under the name of "African philosophy," this cohort of scholars set out to try and delimit the real boundaries of philosophy and "to construct a new space for theoretical production" (Hountondji 2002: 177) on the ashes of what they regarded as unwanted undergrowth. In other words, they set out to clear the ground in order to allow for the growth of genuine African philosophy and to give it a better chance in a world in which all the odds were stacked against it. The seed they planted has yielded fruits that continue to nourish the curiosity of younger generations. To this end, their fire was of absolute importance.

On the other hand, fire does have a downside: it is an *indiscriminate* tool of forest management. The range and amount of what is lost in the process of burning is always a worry for those serious about preserving species variety, biodiversity, and ecological balance. What we want to take from the analogy is that in this clearing, in this making room for new growth, the potential loss—or even extinction—of species variety should never be discounted. In hindsight, perhaps the all-out war to deprecate and decimate almost everything perceived as ethnophilosophical in character represents the other side of this philosophical fire. In his reflections in the book *The Struggle for Meaning,* which features as a sequel to his earlier work, Hountondji (2002: 75) provides insight into the task he had set himself, which was: "to clear the field patiently, [and] establish the legitimacy and outlines of an intellectual project that was at once authentically African and authentically philosophy." Of course, there is good reason to doubt whether the field was indeed cleared with the supposed patience alluded to above, especially if one were to consider the statement of declaration with which he opened the critique of ethnophilosophy—that famous sentence "By African philosophy I mean a set of texts, specifically the set of texts written by Africans and described as philosophical by their authors themselves" (Hountondji 1996: 33), a statement which itself became the subject of numerous essays, counter-positions, and subsequent clarifications by the author himself. That is not our main concern at this point, our principal task was to draw attention to the "fire" that was lit and how that may have shaped the field of African philosophy.

Given the centrality of the critique of ethnophilosophy to African philosophy and its outlook today, it is important that we devote some time to examining the influence that this has had on the discourse of African philosophy. The critique of ethnophilosophy is a subject that has become synonymous with one of Africa's most celebrated philosophers, Paulin Hountondji. His critique of ethnophilosophy is not only regarded as a philosophical masterpiece, but it is also a work that is arguably as popular as it is controversial. In the words of Masolo (2000: 152), "Hountondji is not only one of the most prolific African philosophers, but also one of the best and most widely read, and perhaps one of the most controversial. His work may be best known for his critique of what has gained both notoriety and currency as 'ethnophilosophy'." Passing judgement on his own book, *African Philosophy: Myth and Reality*, a collection of essays constituting the critique of ethnophilosophy, Hountondji (2002: 149–50), had the following to say: "The success of the book [African Philosophy] can be measured by some simple indices. The first is that it generated, and to this day continues to generate, bitter controversies. The very ferociousness of some of the criticism is proof that the positions advanced leave no one indifferent." That the book continues to attract attention and that the arguments put forward continue to polarize opinion cannot be overemphasized. However, in recent years two opinions seem to have emerged. On the one hand is a group that feels African philosophy has moved beyond the debate of ethnophilosophy and thus that to revisit it is akin to flogging a dead horse. For this group of scholars, Hountondji's critique pronounced the death of ethnophilosophy as a discourse.[1] This position will stand only if we accept as unassailable the inversion of the conventional understanding and deployment of the name ethnophilosophy to signify something negative and undesirable. However, if the name is "used [rather] positively, [to refer to] a branch of the more general ethnomethodology which is a phenomenological approach to interpreting everyday cultural expressions as a guide to philosophical research into, and interpretation of, socio-cultural contexts of participants' practices and speech" (Masolo 1997: 63), then this can in no way signify a dead discourse. But of course in saying this, we cannot deny that there is little possibility that this term will ever recover from the reputational damage it has incurred. Curiously though, the term ethnophilosophy is not the only term to suffer negatively from this penchant to invert meanings. Hountondji admits to doing the same with the concept of "unanimism." Regarding this term Hountondji (1996: xxv) states the following in a footnote:

> I took the word from Jules Romains, a French novelist of the early twentieth century, who meant something quite positive: the feeling of solidarity with human beings, the doctrine which advocates 'unanimous life' as a means to break free from individual loneliness and create communion within human groups. When I borrowed the word, *I completely inverted its original meaning and gave it a pejorative sense.*
>
> [Emphasis mine.]

Of course, language takes its own liberties, but the point we wish to make is that there can indeed be consequences of a serious nature if the new inverted, pejorative meaning goes on to eclipse and occlude the conventional and original meaning of a term. The possibility of dissuading any interest in exploring the other more conventional uses of the term is real. Let us return to the issue of ethnophilosophy and the other opinion alluded to above.

There is also a second group who feel that since the dust around the critique of ethnophilosophy has now settled, it is perhaps time to take stock in terms of the journey travelled, where we have come from, including not only achievements made but more significantly the opportunities that may have been missed in the process. Although we will revisit this point in the coming chapters, it is important to emphasize that philosophy progresses not so much by celebrating its successes, but by giving itself time to revisit some of its own serious mistakes and failures. In taking a position to open discussion on ethnophilosophy and to invite contributions for an issue of their journal, we have no doubt that the editorial team of the journal *Filosofia Theoretica* share the second position. We are referring here to their January 2019 call for of a debate in their journal dedicated to revisiting the question of ethnophilosophy.[2] Mudimbe (1988: 158) acknowledges that since its publication, Hountondji's book *African Philosophy: Myth and Reality* has become "the bible of anti-ethnophilosophers." It is regarded by its admirers as having pronounced the final word on this matter but—like the Bible itself—the interpretation of its message and its final position have remained sources of major controversy. Moreover, it is important to indicate that this focus on ethnophilosophy is also an opportunity to honor an invitation extended to philosophers by the author himself to start assessing the impact of the critique of ethnophilosophy. As the following passage explains:

> If the critique of ethnophilosophy has had this liberating effect on some, it seems to have had on others a paralysing effect, by preventing them, through excessive scruple or hesitation, from exercising on African culture and experience their talents as analysts and philosophers. It was as if any work on Africa was *a priori* suspect of ethnophilosophical contamination, and that to retain philosophical purity, one had to hover above concrete situations!
>
> Hountondji 2002: xviii

He continues:

> In referring to these types of reaction, one fruitful, the other unproductive, all I wish to do is to draw attention to a problem that would be interesting to study in itself: *that of the impact of the critique*

of ethnophilosophy. It would be interesting to assess this impact using the most rigorous methods, so as to judge the effects of this critique on intellectual productivity, and to determine its proper place in the history of African philosophical research, and in the broader field of Africanist research.

Ibid.: xviii [Emphasis mine.]

It should be clear to all (including, of course, the legion of anti-ethnophilosophers) from the above that the topic of ethnophilosophy is not closed and revisiting it is not a waste of time. In fact, as Janz (1997: 236) correctly points out, "dialogue between different orientations of African philosophy is not a prelude to philosophy, but is philosophy itself." It should be clear also that even the author of the critique himself would wish to see the subject explored, albeit with fresh eyes. It is crucial to assess the impact of the critique of ethnophilosophy in terms not only of its liberating effect, but also the potentially paralyzing effect it may have had on the field. We do not think anybody could possibly doubt the quality of the argument in the critique and the extent of its influence in shaping discourse on African philosophy both locally and internationally. It is now clear to most readers that the critique of ethnophilosophy revolves around the rejection of the following main issues: a) unanimism (the idea of collective philosophy and the insinuation that everyone agrees with everyone else) and b) extraversion, by which Hountondji means the act of being externally oriented or fixated with addressing an external audience instead of ourselves as Africans. These are arguably the most important reproaches that he has directed at all the work he saw as belonging to the category of ethnophilosophy among many other shortcomings. An elaboration of these, something to which Hountondji has devoted a considerable amount of time in responses and counter-responses and of course in dialogue with numerous other philosophers, will not constitute the focus of our discussion. However, it may be crucial to point out that while the critique of ethnophilosophy went a long way toward shaking up philosophers and giving them a jolt of energy to be more critical and circumspect in their writings by taking intellectual responsibility for whatever they put forward, the sting in the original critique has become less potent. Being a topic that has attracted so much debate, it was inevitable that there would be revision and modification of some of the seemingly extremist views. Today we can agree, as Wiredu (1992: 9) points out, that "a volume on Ghanaian philosophy is a volume in African philosophy." And more crucially, that "talk of the communal philosophy of an ethnic group does not necessarily imply that the conceptions involved are entertained by all members of the group. What it means is that anybody thoughtfully knowledgeable about the culture will know that such conceptions are customary in the culture though he/she may not subscribe to it" (Wiredu 1998: 25).

The need for such expository and reconstructive work does not serve the outside world alone—it is not always externally oriented—for these works are as important for satisfying the curiosities of Africans themselves as they are for external readers. Africa is a vast continent and these works on communal or ethnic philosophies serve an important role for Africans even without looking at their role to the outside world. It hardly needs to be emphasized that through this literature (and without leaving our desks), most Africans are able to travel across the continent and also back in time to connect with crucial philosophical insights into the lives and thinking of fellow Africans. On the other hand, it is also important to note that even the so-called examples of ethnophilosophy are critically informative and at no point are they mere collections of communal beliefs, worldviews, proverbs, and sayings bereft of internal analysis even if the thesis defended, upon closer examination, may later turn out to be misconceived. Although he remains critical, Hountondji has had to concede the following regarding the value of the works of an ethnophilosophical nature that he had reproached for being primarily externally oriented and thus serving only to satisfy the curiosities of the outside world:

> It can be assumed therefore that they meet a real need within the African academic community itself and are not just intended for an external audience which means that these works are not as *extroverted* as I initially asserted but at least to some extent an African way to meet

the Socratic demand: 'Know yourself.' In fact, I clearly recognised, shortly after publishing [African Philosophy: Myth and Reality], that such studies were not only legitimate but absolutely necessary.

                                    Hountondji 2018: 11 [Emphasis is original.]

There is no reason for me to elaborate on the position expressed here other than to draw attention to the fact that we continue to read and to listen to arguments today that rely steadfastly on the critique of ethnophilosophy but seem so oblivious of the above expressed position. The main problem has much to do with the high levels of enthusiasm— if not the excessive passion—among some of the strongest followers of the anti-ethnophilosophy crusade and their ability to feed off this populism. And harping relentlessly on selected aspects from the critique by Hountondji that by now are commonplace in African philosophy, they proceed as if any attempt to engage with communal philosophies or particularistic studies of the philosophy of various ethnic cultures is a mortal sin. But the value of ethnographic studies in reconstructing philosophies in Africa cannot be underestimated. As Masolo (2000: 157) points out: "there had been some excesses in the critique of ethnophilosophy that appeared to leave no room for a positive engagement with the ordinary, thus leaving the impression that philosophy was the contrary of the 'ordinary' rather than its clarification, analytically or synthetically."[3] As stated above, the critique of ethnophilosophy enjoys canonical status in contemporary African philosophy for a reason. It has had and continues to have tremendous influence on the way African philosophy has been produced and continues to be produced. The positive outcomes of the critique are perhaps most manifest in the proliferation of high quality publications and works produced and being produced to this day in the aftermaths.

While Hountondji has sought to maintain his earlier position he has also admitted that "[his] critique of ethnophilosophy and [his] rejection of collective thought were, to be sure, a bit excessive" (Hountondji 2002: 129). However, there seems to be little evidence to suggest that many admirers of his critique of ethnophilosophy have been moved to change their views and therefore adopt a more sympathetic position. It is also true that without the benefit of reading his own autocriticism in *The Struggle for Meaning*, it is not unusual to maintain the hard-line position against ethnophilosophy even as the lead figure behind the critique has since taken a more conciliatory position, a position perhaps best captured by Wiredu (2004: 4) as follows: "In this [ethnophilosophy] controversy, Hountondji's dialectical resilience has been much on display. But he has not been averse to revision." In *The Struggle for Meaning*, Hountondji describes how Alphonse Smet, "openly deploring what he saw as a misunderstanding of Tempels, whom he knew better than anyone else, he later through his research completely renewed the study of Tempels to the point that even the latter's most determined critics had to take a more balanced view of the man" (Hountondji 2002: 143). We have no doubt that among those he counts as Tempels's "most determined critics," Hountondji includes himself. Exposure to such views is crucial in terms of reshaping arguments and opinions, although curiously Hountondji still maintains that this additional information has not impacted on his original thesis. In the history of philosophy, we are often implored to read scholars within the context of their time and to understand the circumstances that may have shaped their thinking. Despite acknowledging that his knowledge of Tempels has improved since he wrote the famous critique, the question that remains is: In what sense is it philosophically prudent to maintain, as Hountondji does, that "the criticisms levelled here at *Bantu Philosophy* were and still are justified in their own way" although "they do not, however, fully place *Bantu Philosophy* in the socio-political context of the former Belgian Congo; neither do they relate it to Father Tempels's personal development as a priest and scholar."[4] It is perhaps better to leave it at that.

Admittedly, the critique of ethnophilosophy, henceforth referred to as "the critique," has also been elevated to a magisterial discourse to serve other ulterior motives which we believe were never intended, but that can be is a story for another day. To take a closer look at the potentially paralysing effect of the critique on the development of African philosophy, we shall turn to the Hallen's crucial recollection following its publication. As Hallen (2010: 76) recounts:

At first, virtually no one wanted to risk being labelled an 'ethnophilosopher,' and there is no doubt that his [Hountondji's] critique led, in part, to the extensive period of soul-searching in the 70's and early 80's on the part of African philosophers over how philosophy in the African context should be construed. For the term 'ethnophilosophy' had, for many, become a euphemism for false and anti-African African philosophy.

The situation described in the quotation above was of course a consequence of the appeal within the critique to stop the intellectual crucifixion of Africa. If ethnophilosophy had become a euphemism for false philosophy and anti-African philosophy, it is not very difficult to see how this impacted on how individual philosophers had to respond. The question of African liberation was an emotive issue and remains so. The clarion call no doubt imposed an emotional toll on any who may have contemplated that approach to African philosophy, for one could not do so without at the same time feeling that they were contributing to the intellectual betrayal of Africa. There is no doubt about the existence of consensus around the broader emancipative mission of African philosophy and anything contrary to these ideals was unwelcome. To be a true champion for the intellectual liberation of Africa meant one had to stay away from ethnophilosophy. Ethnophilosophy was thus presented as anathema to the goals of African intellectual liberation. It had become a term of derision despite the fact that in its etymological sense ethnophilosophy—rendered simply as *ethnos philosophia*—carries no such disparaging meaning. Had there been a strict adherence to its etymological meaning, perhaps this negative and in our view repulsive attitude towards ethnophilosophy may not have arisen. To this day, the name still carries the same stigma in the minds of a number of intellectuals.

From what Hallen recounts above, it is evident that African philosophers were held back from, or felt the urge to avoid, any discourse on ethnophilosophy in the name of defending the African cause. The urge to abandon and thus steer clear of and away from anything that would be considered ethnophilosophical no doubt impacted on the development of African philosophy and more crucially on the fecundity of its expression as an enterprise. Part of its paralyzing effect was to trigger a kind of self-imposed intellectual curfew and fear to explore all available intellectual resources in the construction of a practice that was still in its infancy. One could identify this self-censorship where to be a progressive intellectual and scholar meant distancing oneself from ethnophilosophy as a problem that continues to impact the growth of the discipline today, since very little has been done in terms of trying to understand African cultures and from that basis to develop philosophical ideas and concepts based on concrete cultural experiences.

Through the unrestrained bashing of ethnophilosophy and the work of individuals he identified as its champions, Hountondji had managed to invest the word "philosophy" with a certain amount of furtive power, such that to be a true African philosopher, one had be conscious of one's location and place all the time on the philosophical platform. This would invariably induce in the minds of many a form of self-monitoring and self-regulated conformity reminiscent of Bentham's historic ideal prison called the *panopticon*.[5] Of course, there are some who defied this urge and had the mettle to continue with the reconstructive task of elaborating on the philosophical thinking of their peoples, but there were fewer of these. As Hountondji (2002: 175) recounts so interestingly, Sodipo was "in total disagreement . . . with my ideas on ethnophilosophy, he paid a careful, sometimes amused but tolerant attention to them, all the while pursuing his research on Yoruba thought." We bring this up because of the significance it has in understanding the often glossed over salient and subtle distinctions in the approaches to philosophy and its content—a feature which is clear in the works of the first crop of professional African philosophers as a group and one which remains influential even today. The attitude by Sodipo described above confirms an interesting point of distinction between the approaches mostly adopted by philosophers contributing to the debate on African philosophy from English-speaking Africa and that of their Francophone counterparts, although such a distinction is often overlooked partly because of how popular the critique has become. This difference which

is not only grounded in the polemical approach typical in this case—
that is, Hountondji's—is given the most clearest articulation by Irele
(1996) in his introduction to the book *African Philosophy: Myth and
Reality*. His observation reads as follows:

> The sharp polarisation which he [Hountondji] often suggests between
> enthnophilosophy and traditional philosophy in the Western sense is
> absent from the contributions of the English-speaking writers to the
> debate on African philosophy. The latter have tended rather to consider
> the entire field of mental productions accessible to the African through
> his total cultural experience as a legitimate province of activity for the
> African philosopher. Their efforts have been bent towards making
> clear the discriminations that need to be established so as to ensure a
> proper methodological relationship between the different areas which
> may be thought to constitute this general field. Wiredu's position in
> particular seeks a fine mediation between the African and the Western
> traditions of thought in what he calls an 'African practice of philosophy'
> which would integrate individual reflections upon African material,
> upon themes contained in traditional African systems of thought, into
> a comprehensive philosophical enterprise informed in its spirit and
> methods by the canons of Western philosophy. In this way the modern
> African philosopher would be able to take charge, in an all-inclusive
> approach to philosophy, of the heritage of thought provided by his
> particular background while bringing into a meaningful relation with
> the more formalised system of thought of international philosophy.
>
> Irele 1996: 29

In his essay, which is basically a survey of African philosophy and its
development over time, Wiredu (2004) alludes to a similar distinction
as he reflected on why the question and animosity against
ethnophilosophy did not reach the same feverish heights among the
Anglophone African philosophers and with the same aggressiveness
that it attracted among Francophone African philosophers. In his
observation Wiredu (2004: 6–7) states:

> It is an interesting fact that keenness on the critique of ethnophilosophy
> has not been as much in evidence among Anglophone African

philosophers as among their Francophone counterparts.... Among Anglophone African philosophers, the study of communal African philosophies has not evoked any concerted outcry, and works such as Abraham (1962), Danquah (1944) or Idowu (1962) remain highly esteemed, and rightly so. If Mbiti (1990) has been greeted with considerable criticism, it has been mainly because of certain specific things, such as its claim that Africans cannot conceive of a future extending beyond two years.... In fact, the study of traditional communal philosophies is a time-honoured branch of African philosophy, with antecedents in the work of such historic thinkers as Edward Blyden, Africanus Horton, and Mensah Sarbah..... More recent works of high standing in the tradition of Abraham, Danquah, and Idowu are Gbadegesin (1991) and Gyekye (1987).

The point here is that particularistic studies of African philosophy and the study of communal African philosophies are integral to the construction of a tradition of contemporary African philosophy, especially when careful analysis and appropriate theoretical tools are brought to bear on African traditions. It is interesting to note that in an account which recounts his participation at the 1981 Second Afro-Asian Philosophy conference, which took place at the University of Nairobi, Outlaw makes the following submission regarding the different positions held by some of the first crop of professional African philosophers. We shall quote this at length for the value it adds to the contestations that marked the field and which would play a major role in defining the nature of the discourse as we know it today including of course the different attitudes towards philosophy's relationship to the traditional past. As Outlaw (2017: 253–54) recounts:

Among the many fruitful engagements and experiences I benefited from while at the Nairobi conference and in the city of Nairobi, particularly notable were discussions with Hountondji, Wiredu, and Oruka regarding the cogency of the idea that it should be concluded that among 'traditional' African peoples there were, indeed, persons whose reasonings and articulations merited academic philosophers regarding them as worthy instances of philosophizing in keeping with expanded senses and criteria of philosophical effort emerging from giving respectful, though critical attention to articulations by such persons. At issue were the matters of the historical, sociological, and epistemological scope and content of the enterprise being developed that we now term 'African philosophy', the subfield of African philosophy in particular: namely, whether African philosophy should include the articulation of 'traditional' African thinkers (that is, persons who lived prior to the advent of 'modern' formal education in Africa, and those who, subsequently, were not among the beneficiaries of such schooling). Hountondji was adamant in saying 'No!' to such inclusions; Wiredu, soft spoken in his careful thoughtfulness, deciding in the affirmative; and Oruka passionate in joining Wiredu in concluding 'Yes!' (Oruka would go on to produce pioneering field research and publications along precisely this line of inquiry with his studies of 'sage philosophy.' Wiredu, on his own and while collaborating with his Ghananian colleague Kwame Gyekye, [now sadly late] would go on to produce equally pioneering work on the philosophical articulations and significance of instances of thought by the Akan thinkers).

The "Yes" and the "No" represent positions that not only belong to the individuals cited, but to divisions that remain to this day, impacting of course, on whether one takes the traditional thinkers and cultural ideas seriously or whether they have no place in the discourse of modern philosophy. The often assumed clear dichotomy between tradition and modernity with the former being perceived negatively and even as detrimental to the later has compounded the problem. The other interesting thing, were this possible, would be to establish in precise terms the extent to which this "Yes" and "No" has contributed in shaping both the conception and reception of African philosophy outside of our own continent. However, it would seem Hountondji's subsequent work on the re-appropriation of indigenous knowledges now appears to bring him closer to the position of his other Anglo-phone compatriots described above. One might also be inclined to account for the different attitudes towards the traditional African past described above and its relevance to philosophy on the basis of the different colonial experiences and in particular the cultural policies instituted by each of the respective colonial powers and how this may have shaped people's attitude towards their past.

Once ethnophilosophy was rendered a euphemism for "false" African philosophy, it is not difficult to infer how this development could have impacted even the teaching of philosophy in the years immediately thereafter. The period of the 1970s and early 1980s was undoubtedly one of the most important in the formative stages of African philosophy and in its expansion as a university course in Africa. It is also the period when most of the individuals who would then graduate to become teachers of philosophy were at that stage students in the newly formed departments. There can therefore be no doubt around the impact this view of ethnophilosophy had on this cohort of individuals whose philosophical formation took place during that time. Having found it a betrayal to entertain any thoughts of ethnophilosophy and thus turned their back on it, in a way these teachers became the new crusaders in this discourse. They would invariably pass this on to most of the students they taught, making this hesitancy therefore self-perpetuating. The problem is that once something is designated as negative, the chance of it attracting closer and more sympathetic reading is minimal, and the well-calculated choice of epithets to characterize this approach and works did not help either. For that reason, most academic philosophers were predisposed to dismiss most things that seemed steeped in the direction of ethnophilosophical literature or material. By declaring ethnophilosophy a false philosophy, and a means of perpetuating African servitude, there was nothing that would be so unthinkable, so immoral, and so academically unrewarding as following this false and sterilizing route compared to the noble goal of African intellectual liberation. And so to this day there is still evidence of an attitude of inquisitional intolerance akin to fundamentalism against anything that borders on communal philosophy including even particularistic studies that yield the various ethnic philosophies. The ethnophilosophical sin is something that others try hard not to commit, to the point of staying away from any engagement with African traditions including even linguistic or conceptual analysis of those traditions as a basis of African philosophy, given that such terminologies and their meanings are folk in character and origin. They represent collective rather than individualised cogitations. But, and here is the point, "if philosophers" as Appiah (1992: 106) rightly points out, "are to contribute—at the conceptual level—to the solution of Africa's real problems, then they need to begin with a deeper understanding of the traditional conceptual worlds the vast majority of their fellow nationals inhabit."

The bid to literally squash or put an end to ethnophilosophy and its practice was effectively a stranglehold on an alternative conceptualization of philosophy which needed further intellectual investment to find itself. In fact, Solomon (2001: 101) is correct that "our critical scrutiny today should be turned on the word 'philosophy' itself, along with its history, to realize that what was once a liberating concept has today become a constricted, oppressive, and ethnocentric one." There is absolutely no reason why we should be conscripts of a singular idea of philosophy and thus suffocate ourselves, instead of creating room for us to provide an alternative reading of this seemingly sacrosanct concept. It is important to remember, as Hallen observes, that

> The criteria used to define what is and what is not philosophy in the world today are unfairly biased by and for 'philosophy' as presently construed by Western culture. There may have to be *some* common ground if the word 'philosophy' is to continue to have cross-cultural significance. But Africa, in particular, has not received just consideration in that regard. . . . In so many respects, it seems, Africa's cultures have not benefitted from the kinds of exhaustive and empathetic scholarship that are being lavished upon other parts of the world.
>
> 2002: 11

Building that common ground begins with the philosophers from the so-called periphery contributing their own perspectives towards how this activity, which is inherent in all communities, should be conceptualized. There is nothing sacred about the concept of philosophy that it cannot be understood differently—even the sacred scriptures themselves being the purported voice of the Almighty are read and taught in context. It is time for African philosophers to begin to think again in terms of what it means for them to continue to practice philosophy in the footsteps of the dominant Western tradition and whether this is worthwhile if indeed that understanding of philosophy places out of its purview much of what brings out the fecundity of African philosophy as a discourse. The negative attitudes towards indigenous traditions and their ideas comes across as an instance of what Hallen bemoans above: it epitomizes a lack of exhaustive and empathetic scholarship. There is need to rediscover the task of thinking and to see whether the only real task for the philosopher is to be the equivalent of an inquisitor or a witch-finder. It is crucial that philosophers must not become the dangers that philosophy has to be protected from. Yes, it has been shown that "philosophers are rarely as 'unphilosophical' as when they are laying down the law about what is and what is not philosophy" (Bernasconi 2003: 573). Reason is often made subordinate to other whims in this process. Outlaw is correct to argue that "we mislead ourselves if we require that there be something more than 'family resemblances' common to all the instances we recognize as instances of 'philosophy'. . . . There are no transcendental rules *a priori* that are the essential, thus defining, feature of 'philosophy'" (Outlaw 1992: 73). The irony is that in the name of philosophy, African philosophy has unwittingly constrained and constricted itself in a significant way. Reaffirming the position of Outlaw above, Bernasconi (2003: 578) reminds us that "there is no single definition of philosophy that covers even everything that is regularly recognized as philosophy within the academy. The flexibility of the conception of philosophy is what allows each major philosopher to redefine the discipline, often in a way that belittles or even excludes from philosophy much that had previously been included." Could it be therefore that Hountondji seized on the flexibility of the concept of philosophy to redefine the field of African philosophy in a way that disparaged, and even excluded, from philosophy all work that had previously counted as such? This could be what we are looking at in the case of ethnophilosophy.

As we continue to bemoan the fact that the history of philosophy has long suffered from exclusionary tendencies that have kept us from appreciating the contribution of different traditions of this world, we should at the same time never forget to reflect on our own situation in African philosophy. We must look at how prejudices and stereotypes concerning certain modes of doing philosophy are impacting the discipline. When Hountondji (1989: 3) writes:

> Allow me to make a few remarks, in a most direct manner, a clarification of meaning, scope and aim of my criticism of ethnophilosophy. I am forced here to go through an exercise which I do not like; to respond point by point (or 'fist by fist', in line with a joke of a friend of mine whom I cannot mention here) to criticisms which sometimes just look like personal attacks. But I do it with much pleasure, because, beyond these 'ad hominem' criticisms, founded on a strong will not to understand, there are fortunately many others, which do justice to the problems presented and have the additional merit of pointing out real theoretical problems and, from time to time, at inaccuracies and other loopholes in my own formulations,

it should never be lost to contemporary African philosophers that those "real theoretical problems," "inaccuracies," and other "loopholes in his own formulations" are invitations to explore further, in particular how these unintended but "real theoretical problems" and "inaccuracies" could have impacted the developmental path that African philosophy might have taken. Yes, there is no doubt that Hountondji contributed immensely to the field of philosophy by exposing various shortcomings. And yet, as Ochieng (2010: 31) points out, "here again, it is necessary to make distinctions. It is obvious, for example, that Hountondji's thought is bereft of any sustained engagement with African art, literature, music, film and architecture. Such an engagement might have offered him a far more subtle, more complex understanding of the different varieties of *mythos*, and perhaps even tempered his grammacentrism." It is not so much on the theoretical problems or inaccuracies that we need to focus, because much exists already on this, but it is rather the impact of these on African philosophy and how it could have shaped out that we still need to assess in our philosophical reflections. Among some of the potential consequences of the 'real theoretical problems' is surely a deliberate conflation of *ethnos philosophia*[6] with ethnophilosophy in the pejorative sense. We agree with the submission by Afolayan (2018: 11) that "many concepts like ethnophilosophy and negritude have been subject to gross misuse that seems to obviate their significance" but we must never forget that where new knowledge or insight demands it, concepts can be "updated', 'reclaimed', and 'renegotiated' because of their capacity for intellectual reusability."

The history of philosophy in the West differs greatly from how philosophy became an academic discipline in Africa. To begin with, whereas philosophy in the West is considered the mother of all disciplines, meaning that it was there prior to the birth of all the other disciplines as we know them today, the same is not true of African philosophy. Even as disciplines established themselves and therefore sought to establish autonomy from the mother with some even attempting to literally bury philosophy, philosophy has always re-invented itself and has managed to keep its foothold as an integral theoretical tool reflecting, raising, and answering questions at the most fundamental level across disciplines. It has managed to do so in part because as a mother to those now stubborn disciplines, they all carry her DNA—philosophy lives in them all. It is for that reason that philosophy remains foundational to all disciplines. African philosophy did not have this privileged history of being there first—unless, of course, we restrict ourselves to the understanding and implications of the universally accepted viewpoint that philosophy begins in wonder. Taken in this sense, philosophy precedes everything else everywhere including in Africa. But as an academic discipline in Africa, it came way after other disciplines had done a lot in compiling, representing, and misrepresenting African systems of thought and traditions. It announced its arrival on a field that had already been rigged against it and as a result, its journey was marked by all kinds of struggles. The birth of African philosophy as an academic discipline is beholden to other disciplines that came before it, and African philosophy has to take on the responsibility to build itself by not only responding to the outside world but also addressing the whole array of distortions and misrepresentations of African thought undertaken (sometimes in its name) by the disciplines that were established earlier in Africa, such as ethnology, anthropology, and studies of religion. For that reason, even as African philosophy has much to protest about, its hostility against these disciplines has to be measured for they are of service, even if it is to refute most of their findings. How else could we reclaim the richness of the philosophical traditions in Africa without turning to some of the useful written records provided by some of these other disciplines? It is in the process of attempting to put these in the service of philosophy that Wiredu's project of conceptual decolonization becomes not only important but coterminous with the practice of African philosophy. As an acute reminder of the pervasiveness of these distortions, "it is not uncommon to find highly educated Africans proudly holding forth on, for instance, the glories of African traditional religion in an internalized conceptual idiom of a metropolitan origin which distorts indigenous thought structures out of all recognition" (Wiredu 1996: 138). Addressing such problems cannot happen without investing much effort and time to studying the traditional philosophies of the disparate ethnic communities by professional philosophers in Africa. By conceptual decolonization, Wiredu (1996: 136) subsumes two complementary processes:

> On the negative side, I mean avoiding or reversing through a critical conceptual self-awareness the unexamined assimilation in our thought (that is, in the thought of contemporary African philosophers) of the conceptual frameworks embedded in the foreign philosophical traditions that have had an impact on African life and thought. And on the positive side, I mean exploiting as much as is judicious the resources of our own indigenous conceptual schemes in our philosophical meditations on even the most technical problems of contemporary philosophy.

In this way, the contemporary African philosopher is able to engage the existing literature and traditions of his/her heritage and to exercise on them the demands consistent with philosophy as a reflective practice and in the process meet the need to contribute towards expanding knowledge about Africa. For that reason, no material should be out of the reach of the philosopher and bad philosophy still remains philosophy and within it can be found material that speaks to the realities that may still require further investigation.

At the heart of what should or should not count as African philosophy, and how broad or distinct the field ought to be, is the question of identity. It is probably true that what distinguishes the field as African philosophy are the cultural traditions it draws from. There are in the field what we can call popular views and others that are less popular. History has always been a theatre of contestations but true contests exist where there are real alternatives. When Hountondji (2002: 153) states that "popularization has its pitfalls that are not always easy to avoid," he is very correct. The "bible of anti-ethnophilosophers" commands a strong following, but as with any set of followers, there are always among them those who are overzealous. If those individuals happen to be entrusted with the responsibility of nurturing the young into the discipline of African philosophy, then the consequences can be very far-reaching. Here is one such example, written as a testimony by Hountondji (2002: 153) himself: "More amusing still is to read the introductory chapter to a school text whose main title—'Does There Exist an African Philosophy?'—is followed by two subtitles inviting two possible answers: 'no' for the first and 'yes' for the second, and to observe that the first author chosen in support of the first answer is a certain Paulin Hountondji." There is no doubt that what he describes is a negative consequence attributable to the critique and how it has been received, obviously, contrary to what was intended. Irele had already alluded to this problem, partly as a result of the way Hountondji presented his argument. For Irele (1996: 28), "it is possible to consider that Hountondji's emphatic tone betrays him into the occasional simplification or overstatement of his case; [there] is a peremptoriness which, while it corresponds to the strength of his conviction, obscures the finer points of his argument and therefore leaves room for its misrepresentation." The weight of such misrepresentations, including the different ulterior motives that these have been made to serve by our detractors in the world, can be a cause of great worry especially given Africa's own history. The point we wish to make is that, it would be interesting, were it possible, to find out how many similar misinterpretations resulted in position papers, seminars, and lecture notes pronouncing the non-existence of African philosophy that are now in circulation around the world, and in particular to find out exactly which point(s) from the critique of ethnophilosophy favored such grave misunderstandings and why.

Finally, as we conclude these reflections on the critique of ethnophilosophy, it is important to remind ourselves as African intellectuals that universalism is a gift of the powerful to the weak. Universalism is also at the same time "a faith, as well as an epistemology. It requires not merely respect but reverence for the elusive but allegedly real phenomenon of truth. The universities have been both the workshops of the ideology and the temples of the faith" (Wallerstein 1995: 81). There is no better way to reflect on the impact of the critique of ethnophilosophy on the growth and development of African philosophy than to remind ourselves of these cold, hard facts. Inherent in the enthusiastic rejection of ethnophilosophy, which is hastily extended to all communal philosophy, is a certain universalism and scientism that needs no further elaboration. Instead of African philosophy introducing itself as a different and a wholly unfettered competitor deriving its mandate and direction from its own cultural horizon, the quest to measure up to the dominant Western model may have inhibited instead of enhancing the options through which it could have manifested its unique qualities and identity as a philosophy. The opportunity for an unfettered growth, including surprises in store that it could have brought as a philosophy, was thus sacrificed at the altar of conformity and acceptability. It was the philosopher Karl Popper (1959: 19) who wrote, "a definition of the word 'philosophy' can only have the character of a convention, of an agreement; and I, at any rate, see no merit in the arbitrary proposal to define the word 'philosophy' in a way which may well prevent a student of philosophy from trying to contribute, qua philosopher, to the advancement of our knowledge of the world." As we contemplate the future of African philosophy, it is important to revisit this in the sense of continually contributing to the mapping, drawing and redrawing of the boundaries of African philosophy as a living discipline and in the light of our own needs as a continent. At no point should we assume, as Janz (2009: 30) correctly observes, "that maps are neutral tools, even in this metaphorical form, and that the result achieved can convince anyone that territory has been legitimately claimed." Disputes over borders, the criteria of inclusion and exclusion, are themselves the lifeblood that keeps the discipline thriving—it is philosophy itself. If African philosophy is to be true to itself as a philosophy, then it must recognize and accept its own incompleteness. It must thrive to distinguish itself not on the basis of intolerance and arrogant grandstanding but through its openness to "dialogue as productive friction" (Monahan 2019a: 86). Indeed it must be appreciated that "the agenda of philosophy [anywhere] is not fixed once and for all; nor are the ways of pursuing the issues on it" (Schacht 1993: 425). Yes, there might be fun in a philosophical put-down, but in order to fully appreciate the richness and diversity of philosophical expression, it is crucial that we do not lose sight of what Solomon (1999: 8–9) urges which is that,

> the joy of philosophy lies elsewhere, in the co-operative development of ideas, in the exploration of new perspectives, in the creation of visions in which the everyday becomes interesting, even fascinating. Criticism has its place, of course, but criticism is, or ought to be, only a tool for shaping ideas, for expanding our vision. It is not, or ought not to be, an end in itself.

There has been an attempt to distance philosophy from the indigenous and the ordinary and the critique may have played into those hands. Philosophers in Africa, and in response to the demands placed on them by history, cannot abdicate the responsibility to develop ideas, to explore new perspectives and visions that will make the philosophical enterprise richer and more fascinating. It is apparent therefore that the polemics often directed at particularistic studies of African philosophy, and those seen as straying too much close to the indigenous ideas and resources, must be supplanted by genuine conversation to advance knowledge about Africa and to engage with all the different sources of wisdom available to humanity.

Conclusion

Almost every new entrant into the field of African philosophy as an academic study is introduced to "the critique of ethnophilosophy" as part of their initiation into the debate concerning the nature of the discipline. Central as it is to the contemporary history of African philosophy, the critique continues to be a source of controversy among Africanist scholars despite numerous attempts by Hountondji himself to provide clarity on most of the issues, rendering true the assertion that philosophy flourishes in spite of, and because of, controversies. Of course, credit must be given where it is due; philosophy in Africa would never have progressed without traversing boundaries and learning from other traditions of thought. Credit must go to Hountondji not only for his intellectual courage but for his role in raising the discourse to the level where it is today.[7] In saying this, we are also aware of the negative consequences his fiery approach and conceptualization of philosophy had on the discipline. The full consequences of his critique on the growth and development of African philosophy are yet to be seriously studied. Powerful as it was, the critique of ethnophilosophy had both beneficial as well as unintended negative consequences on the development of African philosophy. The former are well-known and documented but the latter are less explored. The critique triggered a certain period of paralysis in the field by initiating some kind of self-imposed intellectual curfew for fear of committing intellectual treason against Africa. There was immense risk attached to the label "ethnophilosopher" and that risk remains to this day. Ultimately, while there is reason to celebrate the critique, there is a sense in which the critique potentially inhibited the self-expression of African philosophy as a new entrant onto the field and prevented it from flourishing on its own terms at a time it could have challenged even the very idea of 'philosophy' as construed by the dominant tradition. Instead of liberating African imagination and opening the horizon of possibilities, as promised, the critique (perhaps unintendedly) subjected African philosophy to a northbound gaze in the search for acceptability. By introducing a form of exceptionalism, and therefore rendering the discipline an exclusive and exclusionary practice, the critique may have robbed African philosophy of its potential for unfettered self-expression as a practice drawing from its own culture and a truly authentic enterprise second to none. Just like the ethnophilosophy it so greatly abhors, the critique of ethnophilosophy—and its extremist position and inquisitional intolerance instead of an even-handed and more scrupulous appraisal—may also be guilty of playing into the hands or pandering to the whims of those who never wanted to see the so-called most sacrosanct discipline, "the highest status label of Western humanism"[8] reconfigured in ways that would have required them to relearn what it meant to do philosophy and to be a philosopher. But of course, the opportunity for Africa is not lost and for that reason our contribution to world philosophies from our perspective must continue in earnest.

African Self-Apprehension

Introduction

As Africans, true self-(re)discovery begins at the level of understanding ourselves, our own history and intellectual heritage; it is about African self-apprehension. This means turning our attention to the internalities of Africa in the sense of raising critical questions about where we are with this process and where this has remained problematic. It should be remembered that this knowing of ourselves is crucial in the broader project of decolonizing philosophy. This chapter addresses problems that are caused by the "excessive scruple or hesitation" to immerse oneself fully in the exploration of ideas and concepts embedded within the African culture itself and instead preferring "to hover above the concrete" for fear of "ethnophilosophical contamination." Retracing the epistemic thread in the fabric of indigenous African cultures is in itself a primary means of meeting the Socratic equivalent—African "know thyself." Out of necessity, the quest for African self-apprehension demands that we also turn our attention to other challenges that prevent us from sharing the fruits of our intellectual labor as a continent. The colonial relationship that binds Africa to the West in a special way has also carved the continent into linguistic regions that, for reasons much to do with colonialism, also call for the cultivation of inter-philosophical dialogue on the continent as an integral step toward a better understanding of ourselves.

Philosophy in Context

To situate the unfolding argument of this chapter within the broader context of debate on the nature of African philosophy, we shall begin with a brief but critical recapitulation of another way of looking at the debate that has brought African philosophy to what it is today. Here we offer an account of what we infer from the way in which the debate has turned out, including of course drawing on aspects of thinking that defined the operationalization of the mission to civilize and colonial conquest. This we shall do without recounting the familiar historical narrative regarding preconceived assumptions that guided the anthropologists and others in their study of indigenous cultures as exotic artefacts and exemplars of what used to be; that is, evolutionary remnants of the earliest stages of human culture. At hand in the history of the encounter between Africa and the West, there was an enabling analytic model characterized by three key elements as summarized by Mudimbe citing the work of the Cameroonian philosopher Eboussi-Boulaga. This theoretical or analytical model is defined by three categories or concepts which are: "derision, refutation-demonstration, and orthodoxy-conformity" (Mudimbe, 1988: 52). Put more simply, in their mission to civilize, the missionaries would apply the analytical model as follows: first, the missionary would, based on existing cultural presuppositions, deploy the language of derision to characterize African beliefs and practices. This is then followed by a demonstration of the rationality, intellectual and moral superiority of the colonizing culture, and finally, by the imposition of rules of orthodoxy and conformity to the new religion. This model was used by missionaries and colonizers in their effort to undermine indigenous belief systems and knowledges in general in order to inaugurate a new religion or epistemic tradition as a superior and rationally grounded practice. This analytical model was without doubt extended to all significant areas of life to assert the moral, cultural, and intellectual superiority of the West at all levels. If fact, given the role played by the missionaries in education in colonial Africa, it was only natural that such a model would become instrumental for the colonial project of mental de-Africanization and colonization, and the subsequent alienation of Africans from their culture. However, and fast-forward, it is our conviction that as Africans took the initiative to rewrite their own story after independence, they found themselves confronted by the question of how to negotiate the consequences of this analytic model, how to work outside it and if that was not possible, how to readapt and possibly redeploy it in a manner that could help them address the negative consequences and problems it had created for Africa. If, as Houtondji (1996: 89) argues, "every philosophical [position] is a reply to foregoing [debates] in the double mode of confirmation and refutation or, better still, as a call for further developments, an appeal to future confirmation or refutation, so that every philosophy [in practice] looks forward and backward [in this ever-evolving story]," it is possible to see a similar process of "confirmation and refutation" at play in the manner the early crop of African philosophers entered into the discourse of African philosophy. There is evidence to suggest that instead of jettisoning the above analytical model completely, a strategic choice was made to redeploy the same model of "derision, refutation-demonstration, and orthodoxy-conformity" in order to respond to Africa's detractors in the form of the literature produced by early ethnologists and anthropologists that denigrated Africa. There is a sense in which African scholars, and philosophers in particular, appropriated and redeployed this same analytical model against Western discourse on Africa and in order to reassert the African's right to reason and title to the philosophical practice. There is perhaps no better way to see this model in action than in the critique of ethnophilosophy, as discussed in Chapter One. Our argument is that it is in the critique of ethnophilosophy more than anywhere else that the apparent inversion of the colonial analytical model and its deployment this time targeted at Western discourse on Africa is exemplified. In his critique of ethnophilosophy, Houtondji seems to have adopted the same analytical model of derision, refutation-demonstration, and orthodoxy-conformity, a somewhat strategic way of seizing the weapon of the aggressor and turning it against its owner. The language of derision was deployed in equal measure to deal with Western discourse that sought to project African philosophy as the direct opposite of the rational, followed by a demonstration of the irrationality of the positions advanced by anthropologist and their subsequent refutation. By strategically brandishing the name ethnophilosophy—a term whose ordinary meaning was inverted into a derisive one—to refer indiscriminately to all philosophical works of an ethnological nature modeled in the image of Tempels's *Bantu Philosophy* and many other colonial ethnologists and anthropologists who had projected African cultures as exotic and their peoples as primitive, Hountondji and others alongside him in this crusade, may have succeeded in readapting the above analytic model into a useful weapon but this time against its masters. It is perhaps true that the antidote is to be found in the poison. What was left was to demonstrate, in equal measure, the intellectual capabilities of Africa through the articulation of a philosophy that would meet the new orthodoxy both in definition and substance. To conclude the action plan, Hountondji went on to declare that nothing would count as philosophy unless it were a scientific discourse, and a methodological inquiry with universal aims; and a metaphilosophy, in the sense of a philosophical reflection on philosophical discourse. By this, the rules of orthodoxy in what was to be regarded as African philosophy had been laid; anything that fell short of or failed to measure up to them would not, strictly speaking and according to him, count as philosophy. It is this measure which would be applied to assess and thus if necessary dismiss what had been paraded as African philosophy, but more significantly it would constitute the basis for constructing a true African philosophical discourse going forward.

Meticulous as this would seem (and of course we have already touched on this in the previous chapter), the redeployed analytical model served us well at the level of refutation but it then ran into some problems at the point of prescribing precisely the same rules of orthodoxy from the Western tradition, in the sense of an understanding of the meaning and definition of philosophy adopted. It left intact the Western conception of the philosophical endeavor itself. This would later turn out to be a major source of controversy. Instead of laying down new rules inspired by our own independent assessment of what constitutes philosophy, there was an apparent unwillingness, if not a total oversight, to exert the same spirit of questioning to the definition of philosophy already in use and one that was prejudiced against Africa. For this reason, a reminder of the question posed by Irele (1996: 8–9) in his introduction to the book *African Philosophy: Myth and Reality*, in which the critique of ethnophilosophy was laid out is apposite: "Is philosophy concerned simply with theoretical matters and second-order questions, or does a definition of philosophy admit of other possibilities that take account of the universal human disposition to apply both mind and imagination to the facts of experience?" No doubt, with this question, one of the main issues at the heart of the debate in African philosophy is clearly outlined. As such, anyone familiar with the debates in African philosophy, and the way different philosophers have approached the practice of African philosophy, would agree that the distinct orientations taken in the discourse of African philosophy are at bottom shaped by individual and collective responses to this question. Even the substance of the disagreement in the critique of ethnophilosophy, including the controversies that ensued and which remain unresolved to this day, have much to do with the conception and understanding of philosophy as articulated above, including the philosophical implications of the question raised by Irele. It is also, as highlighted in Chapter One, the basis upon which accusations of "Occidentalism, idealism, elitism, and aristocratism" have been leveled against Hountondji—accusations which apparently seem to refuse to go away despite the amount of work done not only by him, but also by those who share his views, to respond to the critics. While the analytical model adopted from the colonial anthropologists had been redeployed and turned against itself with undoubted astuteness, it was perhaps the decision to adopt and impose the same rules of orthodoxy as regards the meaning and definition of philosophy without question, that was—and remains—the major bone of contention. At that very point, African philosophy lost the opportunity to challenge and thus rid itself of the authority of a self-serving oligarchy in the kingdom of philosophy, one that to this day stifles genuine democratic reforms toward the celebration of world philosophies. It is this restrictive definition of philosophy, together with a seemingly deliberate negative blanket characterization of communal philosophy as ethnophilosophy and the inversion of the meaning of that term ethnophilosophy into a derisive one with little regard for its etymological meaning, that to this day remain problematic. To malign any type of communal philosophy or any particularistic studies of the philosophies of the various peoples of Africa as not philosophy remains one of the negative consequences of this conceptualization of the discipline. We analysed the potentially debilitating effects of this in the previous chapter. To introduce a sense of how this continues to play out within the landscape of contemporary African philosophy, we will briefly make reference to Wiredu. Here we can still witness the significance of the dispute around the term, its deployment and consequences for the practice of African philosophy. When Wiredu one of the eminent philosophers of our time was asked the following question in an interview article, "Do you agree with Paulin Hountondji's critique of ethnophilosophy? If so, why would you agree with him? If not, can you give us a general perspective on what you will describe as African philosophy?", his response was illuminating, and if what he says does not help to put the whole issue into perspective, then probably nothing will. Wiredu's response was as follows:

> Hountondji and I agree on some issues but not on every issue. A lot of my work will fall under what he calls "ethnophilosophy," that is, my reflections on the Akan, what the Akans think, et cetera. That is the kind of thing he calls *ethnophilosophy*. So there is a disagreement there between me and Hountondji because I think that you can do worthwhile work while studying the worldviews and also the philosophy of a whole group of people, especially if they don't have a written tradition. I am not aware of a written tradition in Ghana dating back to, say, even the seventeenth century or earlier, so that is all right.
>
> Eze and Metz 2015: 86

Of course, he goes on to articulate that philosophy must be critical, and to all professionally trained philosophers, that is beyond dispute. However, our point in drawing attention to this response from Wiredu is to address a particular rashness with which certain commentaries and commentators on African philosophy try to demean particularistic studies in African philosophy, sometimes (and ironically) with appeal to Wiredu, even as he demonstrates through his own work not only the way, but also the *value*, of such particularistic studies in modern African philosophy. In a recent book that is probably the first dedicated reading of Wiredu's work, Hallen (2021: 95) is very clear that those familiar with the latter's oeuvre would know that in his work in and on African culture, "Wiredu is concerned, among other things, to confront and disprove accounts of a 'traditional' African intellect that could produce little of philosophical merit. He does not do this on the basis of rhetoric. He does it via subtle and exacting analyses of Africa's indigenous cultures to demonstrate that their languages, beliefs, and practices are reasonable and have philosophical merit." His is a philosophy that demonstrates how philosophy can feed off the indigenous African culture by paying closer attention to its particular set of ideas, concepts, and beliefs and analysing them for their insight and philosophical import. At this point it is also salutary to draw attention to another significantly productive way of looking at African philosophy; that is, African philosophy as hermeneutical. As Oguejiofor (2009: 83) argues, following in the same line of reasoning as Okere and Serequeberhan, African philosophy "must also be a hermeneutics of the African condition, symbols, culture, language, history, and so forth." As a hermeneutical process, philosophy "must be colored by the particularity of its birth." It is at best, as Ramose (2005: 145) points out in an essay with the same title, "a particularist interpretation with universal appeal." The idea of "pure philosophy, pure reason, in the sense in which it is completely non-contextual, is an illusion" (Oguejiofor 2009: 84). In this work, we adopt a similar position and entry point into philosophy where interpretive or hermeneutical studies into the cultures and traditions and lived realities of the African peoples is not only desirable, but is one productive approach in the reconstruction of African philosophy. This aside, the decision alluded above to align African philosophy with the Western orthodoxy, and to adopt that conceptualization as given, may have also ultimately impacted on the ability of our philosophy to manifest in its own way. In other words, the major point of contention in African philosophy has been and remains the possibility of articulating a philosophy that is not bound by nor "grounded on 'Greece' and all that the metonym implies" (Mukandi 2019: 162). Even as it tries to be truly universal in the sense of being able to speak not only to Africa's problems, but to the problems of humanity in general, African philosophy cannot overlook the significance of its own history and culture as a practice. First and foremost, it has to strive to render itself a truly African discourse and that entails paying attention to the fecundity of its own philosophical expression, including how this can contribute not only toward reworking our understanding of philosophy, but also toward the corrective reconfiguration of the philosophical enterprise itself.

That said, it is important that in this chapter and indeed in the rest of the book, our position is made clear that adherence to a particular model of philosophy—such as the dominant orthodoxy or model endorsed by the West—is restrictive and, to borrow the words of Irele (1996: 27), "it excludes from the purview of philosophy those other areas of mental activity in which are engaged the deepest responses of mankind to experience and which cannot but add a vital dimension to the theory and practice of African philosophy." Accordingly then, our task is to contribute to the construction of a tradition of philosophy in Africa characterized by, in the words of the African philosopher Wiredu (1996: 114), a "dialectic of diverging schools of thought with the excitement of an inevitable variegation of insight" and perhaps endless duels of productive friction. To come to grips with the promises of African philosophy, we must begin by acknowledging and accepting the basic fact that the field of study called African philosophy, as well as its demarcation, are not set in stone. Its contours must continue to be negotiated and renegotiated as a living philosophy and that includes its methods, articulation, and exposition. African philosophy must be an embodiment of intellectual virtues, including the freedom to imagine, to create, and to express; it must truly reflect the different modes of thinking by those who never fathomed that one day they could pronounce on their own reality in their own way. We should never postpone asking or answering two key questions: Is there anything distinctive we can bring to philosophy from our history, culture, language and traditions? And second, what, in Africa, is the teaching and writing of Western-style philosophy for? (Appiah 1992: 90). African philosophy should have within its purview "particularistic studies" of the thinking of Africa's ethnic communities.[1] Elsewhere we have argued that the intellectual heritage of Africa should be conferred with the immortality that other classical ideas across the world enjoy through reconstructive writing, which makes it possible for future generations not only to dialogue with this heritage but to innovate it as well (Mungwini 2017: xi). If it is accepted that as it progresses, philosophy constantly returns to its history, and in so doing help to carry that history with it into the future thereby immortalizing some its lead figures, ideas, theories, and insights, it should be apparent to Africans that part of that intellectual history has to be transformed from its oral existence into the written through the critical reconstruction of the various ethnic philosophies on the continent (where this is still possible). It therefore follows that one integral aspect in the study of African philosophy is that of rewriting our history so as,

> to set the defective aspects of the historical *status quo* aright, so that the authentic image and genuine roles of Africans by birth as by other associations or qualifications will properly and honourably appear. This is only being true and just to history made by Africans as by others within and without Africa. In conducting their historical essay, African philosophers want to rectify the historical prejudices of negation, indifference, severance and oblivion that have plagued African philosophy in the hands of European devil's advocates and their African accomplices. African historical investigations in philosophy go beyond defense, confrontations and corrections. They are also authentic projects and exercises in genuine scientific construction of African philosophy concerning the diverse matters of its identity and difference, problem and project, its objectives, discoveries, development, achievements and defects or failures.
>
> Osuagwu 1999: 25

Critical engagement with the traditions of a culture is not synonymous with a fundamentalist rejection of what is traditional. It can be argued that there is a temptation—which perhaps belongs to philosophy in general—to go about the business of philosophy as iconoclasts, swinging our hammer of destruction sometimes indiscriminately in the hope of dismantling what we may perceive as inappropriate beliefs or submissions. This spirit is also true of us in Africa as bona fide members of an argumentative species. And so, as Hallen (2002) pointed out, there have been very few empathetic studies of traditions in Africa compared to elsewhere and in this we must see ourselves as the chief culprits. In the previous chapter we alluded to the existence of those who think they are doing Africa a favor by vying for a philosophical practice that should rid itself of any cultural contaminations and in a manner they believe is commensurate with the demands imposed on them by their training as professional philosophers. Nevertheless, what they may not be giving due regard to is the fact that the indiscriminate process of destruction and demeaning of African traditions is not what makes one philosophically sophisticated or even astute and neither is it in any way novel—it is a continuation of what Africa has suffered since colonial conquest, except that this time the actor is different. Instead, it is the careful reading of those traditions in the sense of treating them as texts that, following the principles of philosophical historiography, ought to be read and critically understood in order to distil their substance and meaning. The traditional African culture and all its paraphernalia is itself a philosophical text which is yet to be fully explored both in terms of the breadth and depth of insights embedded within it. Addressing himself to issues of philosophical historiography, Gracia (1992: 26) makes the following crucial submission: "When we confront a text not written in a language we know, the meaning of the text has a status of a mystery.... We could capriciously assign meaning to the [text] but we do not do it because we know that the text is a product of some other human being's attempt at communicating a message, and we want to find out what that message is, not to project our ideas into the text." This principle of historiography was not observed in the West's many encounters with African cultures and in particular with reference to the need to engage hermeneutically with the cultural traditions that constituted this critical text. This same attitude is inexcusable when exhibited today by Africa's own philosophers. To this day, Africa still struggles under the weight of distortions and misrepresentations that now threaten to concretize into "new truths" about ourselves and which have prompted philosophers such as Wiredu to call for conceptual decolonization as an integral corrective instrument to accompany the philosophical project in Africa. Part of the real tragedy is that today, a huge amount of the misrepresentation of African ideas and traditions has its roots in colonial scholarship. It will take serious dedication, in-depth knowledge of, and penetrating insight into Africa's cultures to be able to deal with this sort of malady. The amount of conceptual damage caused by years and years of mischaracterization of African thought, in terms of foreign conceptual categories, is enormous. What needs to be shown instead is not how effective we can be in adding to this already huge pile of distortions, but rather how meticulous we can be as philosophers in sifting through what remains of these traditions and utilizing the usable aspects to reconstruct a tradition of thought that is African. "The test" Wiredu (1980: x) declares, "of a contemporary African philosopher's conception of African philosophy is whether it enables him to engage fruitfully in the activity of modern philosophising with an African conscience." No doubt, with the help of our knowledge of African languages and culture and utilizing the various tools at our disposals, it should be possible to proceed with this process of reconstruction by identifying and correcting the distortions and misrepresentations. The task of recovering lost meaning, to reimagine and to rebuild, is important in this effort to find our path to intellectual independence. The first crop of African political leaders who had the opportunity to lead Africa at independence may have had many personal shortcomings, but one thing that can never be taken away from them, and here we agree with Wiredu (1996), is their desire to build from our resources and to our design. Their ability to see the practical importance of philosophy and the value of authentic liberation should also inspire the contemporary practice of African philosophy. Without a good grasp of the communal philosophies of the various indigenous ethnic groups on the continent—that is, without this historical record—conceptual distortions that have their origin in the era of colonial anthropology as the handmaiden of the colonization project will remain intact and these falsehoods will continue to be encrusted in layers and layers of more untruths and half-truths which, with time, will concretize to constitute the 'new truths' about us.

In this work, we maintain that the riches of African indigenous ideas and thought are beyond dispute and therefore that fecundity and a multifaceted mode of expression must be allowed to flourish. This fecundity cannot manifest if our conception of the philosophical remains strictly narrow and therefore exclusionary. As Bernasconi (2003: 578) argues, "philosophical debate in the twentieth century has often been conducted by refusing to share the title 'philosophy' with one's intellectual opponents, but the relative flexibility of the conception of philosophy does not have to be used only as a way of narrowing what counts as philosophy. *It can equally well serve to expand its boundaries*" [emphasis mine]. A broader and more inclusive conceptualization of philosophy, capable of reflecting the various manifestations of this practice in different cultures across time, is important. For example, the willingness to pay attention to the "self-expressed forms of life"—the manner in which both art and science are woven into the fabric of African life is important. As Bell (1989: 375) argues, the songs, poems, and even folklore deriving from culture are "part and parcel of the memoir that philosophy must write; they are part of the conversation, both oral and written, that Africans must keep going in a creative fashion." The self-expression of the deepest values of a people are also found in the 'iconic traditions of its culture. Drawing from the work of Soyinka (1976) on an "iconic tradition" in Africa, Bell (1989: 376) argues that part of the narrative consciousness of a culture is its aesthetic consciousness, and this aesthetic consciousness is expressed through its iconic traditions.

At the center of the argument for the decolonization of philosophy is a recognition that philosophy as a practice has been colonized and part of that is expressed in how it is conceptualized. As Monahan (2019: 13) correctly points out, "many of the figures and traditions that have been historically excluded from philosophy 'proper' have engaged in the practice of philosophy in markedly different ways from the European norm, [and this includes] the oral traditions of precolonial Africa and the Americas, for example." At the risk of stating the obvious, writing is crucial to philosophy, but it has not always been the chief means of expressing and capturing thinking. And since developments of the colonial era have impacted on many of the ways in which the colonized organized and expressed their ideas, if we are to get a better sense of the philosophical ideas, then our interest must extend to cover this shift as well. For it is also the case that, "during the colonial period and after, thinkers from colonized communities, excluded from the academy and from established philosophical traditions, turned to fiction, autobiography, poetry, and art (painting, dance, sculpture, music) as the media through which to express their thought" (Monahan 2019: 13). It needs no further stressing, therefore, that if philosophy is to be decolonized and if we are to change our understanding of what it means to do philosophy as part of this decolonizing endeavor, then philosophical practice must be transformed significantly to show this diversity and move away from its narrow conceptualization as provided in the dominant Western tradition. In adopting a flexible conceptualization of philosophical practice, the world loses nothing but instead it is able to reclaim part of the rich oral heritage that exists in so many cultures which can then be judiciously explored for its philosophical ideas and insights. It should never be forgotten that the riddle of life and existence, which philosophy aims to uncover and explicate, is embedded in culture and it expresses itself in many ways—including through art and religion. And these too deserve the attention of contemporary philosophers everywhere, including ourselves.

Liberation and Self-(Re)discovery

It is recommended that one should go back to one's own roots and sources. The sources, the headwater region of creative and original thought, are one's own culture. No familiarity with the foreign and borrowed element can suffice for the articulation of something so deep-felt as one's understanding of one's self and one's world. It is not only a question of fruitlessness when one undertakes to think foreign to oneself. It is also a moral question of being honest and true to one's self.... For black African philosophers it will mean familiarity and identification with their culture. Such identification will enable them to articulate authentically at that ultimate level of meaning which is properly the philosophical, the peculiar understanding of life and reality which their culture embodies.... This self-interpretation which is also a self-assertion, is no doubt the best way to restore self-confidence to a humiliated culture.

                                                    Okere 1983: 118–19, 128

In this submission, Okere articulates what in our view are the reasons why the African philosopher should never regard intimate knowledge of their history and culture as an inconvenience that they can do without. It is this knowledge which will "enable them to articulate authentically at that ultimate level of meaning which is properly the philosophical, the peculiar understanding of life and reality which their culture embodies." It is therefore a matter of great concern as we reflect on the condition of philosophy within Africa that, despite the abundant evidence of the close synergy between philosophy and geography or location, some philosophers seem reluctant to return to the "headwater region of creative and original thought," which is one's own culture to mine the wealth of philosophical resources including orature, that is, indigenous oral literature as authentic literature. Perhaps Bernasconi (1997a: 191) has diagnosed correctly that this hesitancy might be prompted by a fear that Africa might once again be confined to the prephilosphical, but this fear must evaporate once "it is recognized that all philosophies draw on prephilosophical experience, the old dream of a scientific philosophy is *ausgeträumt*, it is exhausted." In fact, "the pretensions of a conceptual debate that has no need to admit the historicity of its own reasoning have been stalemated" (Margolis 1995: 9). The place where the activity called philosophy is carried out matters. For as Janz (2017: 156) makes acutely clear,

> Geography is not just about land or location on a map. It is about what happens and can happen on that land, and how thought emerges and forms in relation to issues such as location ... narratives about belonging and disenfranchisement from place, the memories and hopes about place ... and the specific traditions of thought which have emerged to create and activate concepts which are adequate to a place.

The name and the place called Africa is pregnant with a history, including a range of grievances and priority questions that confer on African philosophy its own peculiar set of problematics. These are issues that arise for African philosophy on account of that history and the place from which the activity of philosophizing is undertaken. To discount this is to lose sight of the contribution that African philosophy can bring to the broader discourse of philosophy.

More often than not, we have come to be accustomed to the description of Africa as one of the richest continents but which, paradoxically, exhibits the worst levels of poverty in the life of its peoples. This economic anomaly is also unfortunately true with regard to knowledge, including philosophy, on the continent. African philosophers have not been able to put their own stamp on philosophy in a way that challenges the very sense of what it means to do philosophy, including the understanding of philosophy itself despite the abundant philosophical riches. This in part because we seem to treat our abundant sources of philosophy with circumspection on the basis of a particular conceptualization of philosophy. For that reason we have remained slaves, and indeed, faithful slaves to a particular understanding of philosophy as a special enterprise divorced from the local, the oral, and the ordinary. There is a hesitancy or reluctance to feed, to nurture, and clothe philosophy with what is local and indigenous and to give it a truly African identity—in this we are, as Africans, complicit in continuing to render philosophy somewhat foreign to our circumstances. In so doing, we are therefore partly responsible for perpetuating the problem of epistemicide in Africa. To account for this apparent paradox of 'the poverty of the rich,' one can probably point to numerous other reasons, but here we shall select only two for analysis, namely: the self-defeating attitude and circumspection towards philosophical resources in our culture; and the existence of linguistic prisons which prevent most Africans from being able to access and therefore share the fruits of their intellectual labor as philosophers. Of course, the later handicap has both indigenous and foreign roots. To the first problem, we use the code name "self-betrayal" and for the second we adopt the term "linguistic handicap" (Mungwini 2019a: 75). While there are indeed complex reasons that may explain what triggers this "self-betrayal" on our part, the focus is on our own responsibility for the problem and what we can do to address it. Once we are able to identify our own complicity (and thus assume responsibility) we shall be able to avoid two common pitfalls: first, a form of fatalism or pessimism that gets us nowhere; and second, trapping ourselves in that tendency, in the words of Hountondji (2002a: 504), to "reject onto others the responsibility for all our misfortunes and misdeeds." Perhaps a balance has to be struck between the historical circumstances that brought us to where we are and the imperative this places on us to seize back the initiative and regain control over our own destiny. By the term "self-betrayal" we wish to capture that sense of "unwarranted hesitation" from engaging fully with reference points and ideas arising from within the African culture itself and preferring rather to hover above the individual concrete cultures for fear of "ethnophilosophical contamination" and in order to retain the much-vaunted philosophical purity. These, no doubt, are signs of an "inadvertent Eurocentrism" (Dussel 2013: 14) within ourselves that we ignore at our own expense. As explained in Chapter One, the fear of ethnophilosophical contamination, which causes some to recoil from cultural resources like orature that by Africa's own history constitute a rich source of ideas, is palpable. To this day we continue to see the label ethnophilosophy used as a stick with which to beat opponents. But the question that all too often is not asked is: Who benefits from Africans shying away from engaging, fully focused, with the cultural and intellectual resources of their own culture? Who should be doing it for them? Whatever way you want to look at it, Africa is the major loser, but the world loses out too. To draw attention to this unfortunate situation, we will turn our attention to a position catalogued so eloquently by Hallen (2002: 11–12) in his book, *A Short History of Africa Philosophy* (and here we shall quote him at length):

> There is yet another dimension to the history of philosophy in Africa—the virtual mountain of historical texts, still incompletely catalogued, that have been indiscriminately labelled African 'oral literature'. For it certainly is the case that academic philosophers were for long predisposed to turn up their noses at the suggestion that an anonymous corpus of writings that included myths, legends, poetry, and proverbs was truly worthy of the title 'philosophy'. One thing upon which Africana scholars and intellectuals largely agree is that the criteria used to define what is and what is not philosophy in the world today are unfairly biased by and for 'philosophy' as presently construed by western culture. . . . But Africa, in particular, has not received just consideration in that regard.
>
> That cultures which were significantly oral in character, or somehow different in other respects, produced forms of literature which are not conventional in present-day Western culture need not mean that they are lacking in philosophical content or substance. In so many respects, it seems, Africa's cultures have not benefited from the kinds of exhaustive and empathetic scholarship that are being lavished upon other parts of the world. The oral literature of the African continent, therefore, has not even begun to receive the attention it merits. Elements of that corpus such as Ifa divination literature . . . *The Ozidi Saga* . . . *The Myth of the Bagre* . . . and the *Song of Lawino* . . . are just four random selections out of the literally thousands of monumental expressions of ideas that deserve careful consideration and analysis before they can be dismissed (as has effectively been the case) as quintessentially 'religious,' as quintessentially 'mystical' or 'mythical,' as quintessentially *non* philosophical.

Why is this so? Part of answer lies in what Hallen points out, which amounts to saying for anything to be properly considered philosophical, it must meet the singular criterion put in place for philosophy by the West. The situation described in the second section of this quotation is reminiscent of the point made by Monahan above. In this submission, Hallen sheds light on the prevalence of a serious anomaly; an injustice that should not be allowed to persist in Africa. An entire corpus, which deserves careful attention and analysis, finds itself shunted into the background or completely neglected despite the fact that within it lies the promise of an epistemic thread linking Africa's oral past and the literate present. How would one possibly explain this shying away from cultural resources by Africans? Perhaps the situation described above can be seen to have arisen in two ways: first, as a result of an ill-conceived attempt to protect oneself from meddling in what is seen as outside the province of "proper" philosophy; and second, as a misguided attempt to protect philosophy itself from any perceived contaminants in the form of oral traditions and to help preserve its purity as "the proverbial queen of the sciences." This, of course, is in keeping with a particular view of philosophy and one that has become entrenched in most African practitioners. When one considers these two attitudes, it is apparent that they share a common parentage in the form of what we might refer to as the colonization of philosophy as a practice. As Gordon (2019: 16) points out, constraints on philosophy can take many forms, some of which are paradoxical. If it is indeed true that philosophy is the love for wisdom, then why does it appear as if philosophers do not care about that wisdom? What sustains this indifference towards indigenous oral resources? It is the duty of African philosophers to work through any constraints that may be preventing them from being true to philosophy in its understanding as an unparalleled, unrestrained, and insatiable love for wisdom. In the quotation above, Hallen not only directs our attention to the size of the material resource that is yet to receive our full attention, but he also points us to an injustice that calls for immediate action. There is little doubt that Africa's steadfastness and preoccupation in meeting Western standards of philosophy has been the cause of its asphyxiation as far as the fecundity and multifaceted expression of philosophy on the continent is concerned. Equally significant is the implication thereof that it is incumbent upon African philosophers not only to come to terms with the effects of a particular understanding of philosophy, but more importantly to realize that, in terms of treatment, African cultures have not received "the kinds of exhaustive and empathetic scholarship that are being lavished upon other parts of the world." It is the duty of African intellectuals to remedy that, for if anybody should want to understand African cultures, it is African intellectuals themselves. Our heritage of oral traditions remain either untapped or only insufficiently tapped, owing to a number of reasons some of which have been described here. Their contemporary importance is not a matter of dispute, although this is not matched by the philosophical commitment to mine them and thus contribute through a critical examination of these to the stock of knowledge about African philosophy. In the meantime, it may be noteworthy to point out that in some places on the continent of Africa, "there is a growing tradition of written philosophy which is very conscious of its heritage of oral philosophy," such as contemporary Akan philosophy, which Wiredu (1996: 133) points to. And one could certainly add to that mix the Yoruba and Oruka's Sage philosophy as evidenced by the industriousness with which experts in that culture have produced philosophical treatise based on the intellectual and cultural resources of the different ethnic groups in their part of the continent. Similar efforts may be found in other places in Africa—Ethiopia—but the same cannot be said about many other parts of Africa. The academic pursuit of African philosophy as "an intellectual exercise that had, has, and deserves a place in Africa's indigenous cultural heritage" (Hallen 2021: 2) in the manner demonstrated by philosophers such as Oruka, Wiredu, Gyekye, Hallen, and Sodipo among others is an issue that should serve as an example to many on how to engage with these traditions and at the same time demonstrate that Africa's cultural and linguistic resources are regarded as valuable resources of philosophy, just as the cultures and languages of other peoples play a key role in their philosophy. The analytic tradition in philosophy has distinguished itself by the amount of emphasis it places on understanding language and meaning as integral to philosophy, and that quest must extend to all languages including those of Africa.

It is of primary significance that any skills acquired at the international level are utilized to grow a tradition of philosophy that speaks to Africa's problems and has its roots anchored firmly in the culture. Within that vein, and concerning the "virtual mountain of oral literature" at our disposal, recourse to such methods as hermeneutics will enable African philosopers to, in the words of Hallen (2002: 61), "work with such ethnographic materials to render them philosophical by interpreting them—distilling and assessing their meaning(s), their true significance(s), and their value(s) to and for Africa's cultural present and future." In contemporary African philosophy, the application of the hermeneutical method was advocated by Okere and taken to new levels by Serequeberhan, among others. Hallen's "virtual mountain of oral literature" is what Okere terms the "reservoir of cultural philosophemes from which any future philosopher can inspire himself or borrow his share of philosophical material. In such a culture a philosopher can plant his roots and from inside it, and as forming part of it, develop a philosophy with his culture as non-philosophical background." (Of course, we must point out the need to insert, without fail, the missing gender pronoun in this citation to reflect philosophy's own commitment to parity of recognition.) The apparent hesitation to engage with oral literature for whatever reason is thus unfortunate because part of the Africanness of philosophy should surely come from this "insertion into culture" as a basis from which to begin our philosophical reflections. Through the method of hermeneutics, oral literature (orature) is approached just like one opens an envelope—to expose its contents and to find out the real message within them. African cultural symbols are pregnant with meaning. A reflection on these symbols, with a view to making the implicit meanings explicit, would contribute immensely to the discourse of African philosophy. After briefly tracing the pattern of the historical development of

Western philosophy and that of Indian philosophy, which are themselves two distinct traditions, Okere (1983: 127) arrives at the conclusion that the mere existence of "various oriental traditions genuinely philosophical is itself sufficient proof of the possibility of philosophical traditions different from the West." And it exposes as ill-conceived the supposed "necessity to graft African philosophy to the Western tradition in order for it not to become an abortive enterprise" (Ibid.: 127). The catalyst in the development and growth of African philosophy lies in its ability to refuse perpetual tutelage and in being able to borrow from others only what is important in advancing its own cause. It is our hope that going forward, Africa will strengthen the need for culturally grounded philosophical reflections. In this way the curse of self-betrayal that continues to haunt Africa may be exorcized once and for all. To reiterate the point, African philosophy must take shape around the struggles of its people, and these struggles are also "expressed by and lived through the 'songs, [myths], poems, and folklore' of its people. We must "reclaim part of the richness of an oral heritage that continues to play a role in the historical struggles that is the post-colonial experience in Africa" (Bell 1989: 378) and realize that such a heritage contributes to our understanding of African reality. It is perhaps for this reason that there may be good reason, in the words of Chitando and Mangena (2015: 226) "to pay attention to developments within specific African [regions] in order to highlight themes that emerge in well-defined contexts," but this of course, without losing sight of the broader African philosophy framework. Pointing to the multiple "dimensions of African philosophy," Wiredu (2004: 21) singles out traditional African philosophy for its "multifarious media of expression." Access to it can be gained through

> communal proverbs, maxims, tales, myths, lyrics, poetry, art motifs and the like. Art motifs are in some ways approximations to writing. In some ways, indeed, they may have a vividness of message that a piece of writing may not approximate. In terms of profundity, this is even truer of some of the deliverances of African talking drums, which communicate abstract reflections through riddles and paradoxes in the very midst of music and dance.

All these invaluable resources of philosophy fall into that category tragically shunted to the background as instances of ethnophilosophy. These are in reality areas of philosophy which have not received attention due in part to a narrow conceptualization of philosophy as an enterprise. Our failure to devote time to delve deeper into this dimension of the living heritage of our traditions can only mean a disservice to ourselves and to the world as well. It should be remembered that every civilization preserves for itself a classical archive from which it constantly draws in order to influence both the present and the future. It is the base from which to launch itself in the march to progress. The injunction "African know thyself" which we have analysed elsewhere in much more detail (Mungwini 2016; 2017a), is an acute reminder of this fact and a philosophical statement on the importance of intellectual liberation and self-(re)discovery. It is a reminder for us to avoid the excesses, if not the tyranny, of a form of elitism which reduces philosophy to an abstract practice that floats above society. Retracing the epistemic thread in the fabric of African culture will not be complete without a considered analysis of oral tradition as a form of literature and a veritable source of philosophy. If this is taken to heart, we may witness as Okere (1983: 129) pointed out, the emergence and indeed strengthening of "alternative philosophies whose complementary characteristics would make humanity richer and the philosophic enterprise itself more fascinating." If there is indeed need to think again, it is about how Africa can invest more effort in mining this "virtual mountain" of oral literature, which is as diverse as the peoples of the continent themselves and from which countless useful concepts on existence and life can be distilled and put to use in advancing other ways of understanding societies and reality in general. Perhaps one of Africa's own failures as far as philosophy is concerned has been the reluctance to embrace the value of fieldwork to philosophy, given that most of the intellectual heritage still lies outside there with the peoples and not so much in libraries and archives as is the case in other places with a long history of written records. A return to Oruka's sage philosophy method in terms of strengthening that fieldwork approach may surely address this shortcoming. Let us conclude this point by saying it is on the shoulders of the contemporary African philosopher that the task to render the "specificities of Africa's various philosophical traditions visible and understandable" rests, and "in [this] reconstruction of the various traditions of philosophical thought in Africa, philosophy, anthropology, and history must necessarily be partners" (Kresse 2002: 33) and not be taken as enemies perennially and ineluctably pitted against each other. The significance of this point is made acutely clear in the context of the practice of African philosophy by Outlaw (2004: 92) when he argues:

> Overall, however, much of this [the inability to utilize the resources beyond the narrow focus on philosophy] has to do with the deformation many professional philosophers suffer as a consequence of our culturally anemic, race-tainted yet race-denying, logocentric, and Eurocentric training. The near exclusive focus, throughout our training, on canonical 'Western' figures and texts as the paragons of 'philosophy,' and the near total exclusion of insights from such disciplines as history, anthropology, ethnology, psychology, theology, sociology, demography, epidemiology, political science, economics, art, music, and dance leave us ill-equipped for working out appropriate conceptualizations to guide us in realizing the promises of 'Africana philosophy.'

As Plant (2017: 16) agrees, the failure to acknowledge philosophy's entanglement in other fields like history and sociology, for example, can only obstruct our understanding of what we are *really* doing when doing philosophy. The mistakes of that intolerance towards other forms of expression are with us today in African philosophy and the losses outweigh the benefits in the sense of how far we could have gone if philosophy had, right from the onset, taken the different traditions, institutions, and cultural expressions like art in its diverse forms as instrumental in fashioning a tradition of philosophy complete with its own approaches and priority questions.

We now come to the second issue referred to earlier above, that is, the problem posed by what we have called the "linguistic handicap" imposed by our historical situation. By this we are not referring to the arguments around the politics of language and by which specific languages should be accorded priority or primacy, nor are we talking about that widely misconceived assumption that African languages are not given to thinking deep intellectual thoughts and that such serious thought therefore requires the colonial languages. Instead, our focus is on something much more pragmatic, a constrictive condition that prevents us from sharing the fruits of our labor across the breadth of the continent as philosophers. Yes, Africa is home to a multiplicity of its own indigenous languages, which does pose challenges of its own, but this is not the issue of concern at this point. For academic reasons we have come to accept, as it stands, the efficacy of operating with a handful of foreign languages despite, of course, the obvious drawbacks related to the problems of having to express one's ideas via a foreign medium. The colonial relationship which binds Africa to the West in a special way has also carved the continent into linguistic regions that for reasons much to do with colonialism also call for the cultivation of inter-philosophical dialogue at the local level (Mungwini 2019a). The production of academic philosophical works has also come to largely follow along those colonial linguistic lines. And so in terms of the professional and academic contribution to the discourse of African philosophy, we have the Anglophone, Francophone, Lusophone, Afrikaner, and Arabic traditions of philosophy on the continent. Few individuals are able to function across all of these languages. Philosophical ideas and insights produced in Africa therefore tend to remain locked away in "linguistic prisons" that militate against dialogue and the cross-fertilization of ideas across a continent still eager to build its own intellectual heritage. Across the world, translation has been used effectively to resolve many of the challenges posed by linguistic differences. As is the case elsewhere, the classical texts in philosophy and other disciplines that are found across the world in our libraries and which are the basis of our instruction in philosophy are mostly translations from Greek and Latin, for example. In contemporary times, much of the works originally produced in the different languages of

Europe (for example) make their way to international audiences through translations. There is no reason for us to overemphasize the role that translation has played—and continues to play—in scholarship, not only in terms of the circulation of ideas but as a catalyst of intellectual innovation and development, something which has helped to bring the world to what it is today. Our concern, however, is with philosophy in Africa and in particular with research results in terms of the literature that is produced on the continent by those involved in philosophy. There is a very strong need for intracontinental dialogue in philosophy in Africa and that dialogue can become vibrant only if we are able to access the ideas produced by fellow philosophers on the continent. For that to happen, translation as a pedagogic practice must become an inseparable partner of the philosophical practice in Africa and that may involve commitment at the institutional level. The few works that have been translated, for example, have been done with outside help, where scholars with a keen interest in having a specific text available to their readership have undertaken the translation and in the process benefited most of us on the continent as well. But we cannot just wait for such chance occurrences if African philosophy is to have the impact we want it to have on the continent, and equally across the rest of the world. In this quest to broaden and deepen dialogue in African philosophy, Africans must take a lead. It must become a priority if our philosophy is to excite the rest of the world and not just those countries to which we are connected via our colonial history. The point we wish to make is that through translation, access to the growing volume of literature produced across Africa will become possible and with it a broader and more comprehensive understanding of its philosophical history. This access will no doubt heighten the dialectic and with it the levels of intellectual engagement as the furnace in which new ideas and insights are fashioned. The philosophers who are beneficiaries of that exposure will not only be more knowledgeable about Africa and its thought traditions, but they will become even more agile and able to contribute meaningfully in terms of boosting Africa's input to the global platform. Even as we advocate translation as an instrument to metaphorically bridge the linguistic divide, a tool with which to open the horizons of knowing, and a means to enhance access to philosophical resources kept out of reach from many on the continent on account of the language differences, we are not oblivious to the challenge this poses. To begin with, translation is a problem that is itself in need of a solution. There is always the danger of a loss of meaning and a further ostracization of indigenous languages if they are not considered as meriting translation. The challenges posed by translation can be acute particularly in a discipline such as philosophy. However, that has never stopped translators from contributing to the dissemination of philosophical ideas by making them available in many languages. The article by Ree (2001) on "The translation of philosophy" raises crucial points. As he puts it,

> But of all kinds of translation, none is trickier than the translation of philosophy. In the first place, there is the problem of obscurity. Philosophical writing, though it may always have clarity as its ideal, is famous for its incomprehensibility.... the canon of philosophical classics includes 'passages, and even whole works, that are obscure.' [citing Roman Ingarden]. ...we may pore over a philosophical argument for months, years, even decades, but in the end be forced to admit that 'we simply do not understand.' It is not the fault of our poor underpowered brains, though; the problem is, as Ingarden put it, that the passage is 'truly' and 'objectively' obscure. And in philosophy, alone amongst the theoretical disciplines, obscurity may be precisely the quality that makes a work classic: it indicates not that the text happens to be inadequately worked out, but that is a sensitive and perhaps artfully elaborated documentation of an essential intractable enigma, an exemplary embodiment of the bafflement in which philosophy takes its rise. Readers will turn to it again and again, like climbers to a very difficult rock face. We try desperately to conquer it; but we would prefer to fail after much trouble, than to succeed effortlessly, since the real purpose of the engagement was to renew our admiration for the difficulty. We would be impoverished, not enriched, if the obstacles were all removed, and we found a clear broad highway spread before us at last.
>
> Ree 2001: 226–7

The beauty of philosophy may be in the enigma and the satisfaction that one derives from the amount of mental effort exerted to finally arrive at what would come close as the intended meaning of the author. Constant interrogation, competing interpretations, and variations—including the potential implications to be drawn from each different interpretation—are the fuel that ignites philosophical hunger, it is what keeps the discipline alive and the enterprise going. It seems therefore true that one characteristic feature of philosophy is its obscurity and abstruseness. Philosophy is by its nature complex, lending itself easily to varied and contentious interpretations and, given the divergence in opinion that may arise as these are debated, it may actually be more detrimental than beneficial to champion translation as a partner in the practice of philosophy. Nevertheless, our view is that while philosophy can be complicated, that complexity should not preclude its being translated. Instead, translation may be the only means by which that complexity can be made available to more minds and thus elicit more responses, in the process helping to resolve some of its most difficult puzzles. The benefit to be achieved from translation, even if some aspects remain contentious, far outweighs the risk of mistranslation. In African philosophy, for example, many of the works by Francophone African philosophers—including Hountondji's extremely popular book, *African Philosophy: Myth and Reality*—has come to English-readers like myself courtesy of translation and the same should be true with regards to works by Anglophone philosophers for our Francophone brothers and sisters. There is no doubt that were this practice extended to include other languages, even those indigenous to Africa where such texts exist, translation will help to encourage more dialogue and fruitful exchanges of ideas, leading to the production of richer and more comprehensive philosophical literature. As a means to an end, the use of translation may therefore go a long way in helping to establish a robust philosophical tradition capable of standing its own on the continent. Enhancing philosophical conversations in Africa across the language divide through translation is one way to increase our philosophical knowledge of the continent. It is also one way by which, to borrow the words of wa Thiong'o (2013: 162), "Africa can add originality to the wealth of human knowledge." This will no doubt be good for Africa and indeed for humanity.

Having considered the two issues that may stand in the way of producing a philosophical tradition defined by a conversation that arises out of Africa's own historical and cultural circumstances, it is important to reiterate that African philosophy, as part of the knowledge production initiative about Africa, must ultimately help the continent find its own path to intellectual independence. The much bigger point we are making here is one that goes beyond philosophy but to which philosophy is an important contributor: it is the question of how to reverse the intellectual marginalization of Africa and indeed the production of knowledge about Africa. This is what we imply in calling for the need for African self-apprehension and it is the essence of the phrase "African, know thyself." African philosophers have no illusions about the importance of staying engaged globally, but a major problem arises from "the inordinate influence of externally generated models" on the African practice of philosophy, to a point where presuppositions about philosophy constrain the imagination rather than liberate it. This is why, as we pointed out earlier in the chapter, the quest for wisdom which is philosophy proper is being held subordinate to a particular conceptualization of the enterprise. To appreciate the diversity of philosophical practice, as (Plant 2017: 5) points out, "one does not have to trawl through the annals of history. The pages of current journals, publishers' catalogues, and conference proceedings abound with discussions of topics that seem eccentric to philosophers of different metaphilosophical persuasions." The borders of philosophy are consistently being probed and they react to contingent factors of existence. We should therefore approach the enterprise with openness in order to grasp, in the widest possible sense, all its complexities and diversities in a manner that is not constrictive, given of course that everything that is considered philosophy is as such based mainly on the analogy of family resemblances. There is no doubt that African philosophy needs to become more daring in the sense in which it addresses itself to the strictures of conventional models and their presuppositions about philosophy in general. There is a need to maintain that consistent urge to reimagine the philosophical enterprise and to look at philosophy from an African point of view—not simply in awe of what others have achieved but from the perspective of contributing Africa's own voice in a manner that will encourage a reconfiguration of the global philosophical platform itself. Before we conclude this point, there is perhaps something that we can learn from the essay by Plantinga (1984) directed at his compatriots and in which he implores his fellow Christian philosophers not just to follow the philosophical trends and topics set by majors centers of philosophy, but to muster the confidence to develop more autonomy and independence to pursue philosophy on the basis of their own priority questions, problems, and guiding prepositions. Plantinga (1984: 256) makes this point as follows:

> The Christian philosopher has his (sic) own topics and projects to think about; and when he thinks about the topics of current concern in the broader philosophical world, he will think about them in his own way, which may be a *different* way. He may have to reject certain currently fashionable assumptions about the philosophic enterprise- he may have to reject widely accepted assumptions as to what are the proper starting points and procedures for philosophical endeavour. And—and this is crucially important—the Christian philosopher has a perfect right to the point of view and pre-philosophical assumptions he brings to philosophic work; the fact that these are not widely shared outside the Christian or theistic community is interesting but fundamentally irrelevant.

> [we encourage the reader to include in their reading the missing gender pronouns]

What he touches on here is the need for more independence and more autonomy with respect to the topics and projects to prioritize including even the widely accepted assumptions about the starting points and procedures for the philosophical endeavour. The pre-philosophical assumptions we bring to philosophy are different for each culture and these should find their way as part of the experiences that shape our thinking. All these are issues that are of huge significance to African philosophers. For Plantinga (1984: 264), the crucial point is that the Christian philosopher "must listen to, understand, and learn from the broader philosophical community and he must take his place in it; but his work as a philosopher is not circumscribed by what either the skeptic or the rest of the philosophical world thinks of theism." Part of the problem with the issue of traditional African philosophy lies precisely in the perception created about African cultures as instances of a relic that deserve to be buried. In so far as our relationship to the cultural traditions is concerned, it remains circumscribed by the fear of ethnophilosophical contamination and our faithful adherence to the dominant conceptions of the philosophical enterprise. Just as Plantinga implores his Christian compatriots, African philosophers need to pursue their philosophy with more autonomy, more independence and boldness just as others in their own cultural settings do.

The determination to know ourselves must yield a distinctive African tradition of philosophy—not in the sense of its techniques and standards of scholarship since critical rigor and interrogation must be maintained at all time—but distinct by reason of its priority questions, its history, its problematics, and background assumptions including projections about achieving a future without epistemic hegemony. World philosophies are the future but only if different traditions and orientations to philosophy—ones that are reflective of the diversity in thinking of which the world is constituted—are enabled to become the new reality. It is within this context that the call "African, know thyself" has to be understood.

Conclusion

There is no question regarding the value of a philosophical tradition in Africa informed by its own culture and constructed as a truly reflective undertaking inspired by all the attendant problematics. Perhaps, more than others, Africa is in a better position, on account of its history, to know the importance of this right to intellectual freedom and self-determination. Even as she seeks to master all the desirable knowledge available to humanity, Africa must within that quest entrench the resolve to engage that world knowledge from its own perspective. In order to do so, it must continue to add to the stock of knowledge itself and part of that knowledge lies in its traditions as a living heritage that philosophers should continuously explore for valuable insights. Success on this front will of course depend on the "degree of dedication to the advancement of an African tradition of thought" that African philosophers are able to demonstrate going forward. And that dedication, we believe, will address among others, two of the challenges highlighted in this chapter. In philosophy, as in politics, every position that can potentially impact the field in a significant way, will attract reactions from those who see a greater future within it and those who view it otherwise. In our attempt to comprehend fully the significance of that position to our field, we should occasionally take time to consider not only the voices of the supporters and dissenters but also the composition of such voices, for it is when the views that we propound appeal to humanity in its diversity that we can be sure that we are contributing our quota in this effort to reconfigure a different world. It is true that one sure way to surrender our own "historic initiative and [thus settle] for the role of a permanent minority and a chronic outsider to the great and yet developing debate of cultures on the meaning of reality and [humanity]'s destiny in it" (Okere 1983: 128), is by reducing our role to that of faithful imitators and commentators caught up in admiration of this world-wide tradition of Western philosophy and its array of great philosophers. To settle for that is not only a failure to realize that all philosophies in this world (including Western philosophy) are culturally generated and therefore forms of *ethno*philosophy that speak to the priorities and questions raised within the context of their own history and place. It will also be a disservice to ourselves and to the entirety of humanity. Hallen (2010: 83) makes clear that "what the West almost succeeded in doing was persuading the rest of the world that its culturally generated 'views' of philosophy—its ethnophilosophy—should be regarded as culturally universal, as forms of thought and knowledge that all other cultures were compelled to imitate if they wished to be admitted as members of that exclusive club known as 'academic philosophy'." We should underline the "almost succeeded," because it is at the same time an important indicator of the amount of effort and resolve shown by other traditions of philosophy in repelling the threat of total annihilation and in defending the diversity of philosophy—a position which is concretizing today into widespread interest in world philosophies. Yes, a great deal can be learnt from Western philosophy but it still has to be "understood as an expression of thinking grounded in *another reality*. To confuse [that] reality with our own simply constitutes a *fallacy of dislocation* [that is,] the fallacy of taking the space or world of another culture as one's own, and thereby rendering invisible the distinct originality inherent in the other reality and its very differences with one's own" [(Dussel 2013: 11) Emphasis original]. We wish to conclude with a note of optimism about the future. To borrow the words of Okere (1983: 129), "despite massive westernisation, it cannot be said that African cultures are about to surrender their identity nor does it seem likely that African children will ever again be taught to speak of 'Nos ancêtres les Gaulois' [our ancestors the Gauls].... the question of a philosophical tradition for Africa different from any other and nourished by the culture of Africa [remains] pertinent." It is within this framework that one has to appreciate the need for African self-apprehension, as this chapter has argued. Philosophy in Africa must help us find answers to the questions of who we are and what we can become historically, politically, and otherwise. It must help us to know ourselves as a people.

Philosophy and Intercultural Dialogue

Introduction

For reasons that will become apparent as the chapter unfolds, we begin our reflections with a question: What can be done in order to be true to both philosophy and to humanity?[1] This question not only admits to a problem in the history of philosophy but also captures a growing orientation in philosophical thinking, one that is increasingly of crucial significance to scholars for a number of reasons, many of which revolve around the recognition that the dominant story of philosophy is unrepresentative of humanity, in part due to its parochialism. Regarding philosophy, it is becoming widely acknowledged that "any reasonably impartial view that surveys the world's cultures find this kind of inquiry into who we are, our experience, and nature of reality widely distributed. And not surprisingly, one finds both broad commonalities in the answers provided to these questions and important intercultural differences" (Edelglass and Garfield 2011: 3). The compulsion therefore to ignore the experiences of particular sectors of society and their thinking, or to even dismiss outright other traditions of thought and cultures, no longer commands wider endorsement by most progressive thinkers and philosophers around the world. That anti-philosophical dogmatic attitude which runs contrary to the very nature of philosophy as a universal human achievement is slowly diminishing in its influence. In an article originally featured in the *Times Higher Education* magazine, Strickland (2018), sums up a position that has been expressed by a number of philosophers and one that is becoming of serious significance to a growing number of thinkers[2] across the West itself when he writes: "There is nothing uniquely Western about humanity's attempt to understand the world and our place in it. Yet prospective philosophy students comparing university prospectuses will quickly find that the vast majority of Western departments completely ignore the long-standing and esteemed philosophical traditions in China, Japan, India, the Muslim world and Africa."[3] It is ironic that most schools of philosophy describe themselves more or less along the lines of being places of "critical intellectual encounter in a globally diverse world," and yet more often than not that critical intellectual encounter is in name only: it is not reflected anywhere in the content of what constitutes the philosophical curriculum. There is therefore an apparent disconnect, if not hypocrisy, between the laudable academic mission statements that spell out the need to create "global citizens" by recognizing the truth concerning diversity of thought traditions in the world and the attempt to keep intact what Davis (2017: 116) has called "isolationist intellectual walls" in the manner in which philosophy is taught in the West itself. The situation captured above becomes seriously worrying (if not disconcerting) when the students in question who are fed on a healthy diet of Western philosophy belong to departments of philosophy in Africa or elsewhere for that matter outside the Euro-American axis. There is no reason to overemphasize the fact that "today there are both compelling moral and intellectual reasons for serious students of philosophy and professional philosophers to expand their gaze beyond a single culture—whether their own or that of some other" (Edelglass and Garfield 2011: 4). A similar point is made by Arisaka (2001: 25) when she makes recourse to the reality that "our world is no longer a collection of isolated nations and peoples but [instead] a dynamic arena of communication and conflict." There should therefore be a concomitant realization by these philosophers for the need to have "fruitful philosophical engagement across cultural boundaries" (Edelglass and Garfield 2011: 3). What emerges from the foregoing is that philosophy cannot continue to be conceived in the exclusivist and narrow manner it has been historically championed without running the risk of being irrelevant to the realities on the ground. The nature of the world today is such that if the spirit of philosophical inquiry is to answer to what it says about itself then it has no option but to concern itself with the "wide variety of voices and standpoints from near and far, all of which focus on issues closely related to human existence" (Kirloskar-Steinbach, Ramana & Maffie 2014: 43). But of course, as Bontekoe (2017) correctly observes, the proclivity to look for excuses and to attempt to downplay the significance of what we have not bothered to investigate ourselves is palpable. Excuses can be made that the world's intellectual heritage is so enormous and that "we philosophers are, after all, merely human—finite creatures, with limited resources of time, energy, and patience. It follows, surely, that we must 'tend to our gardens' and not dissipate energies by pursuing every passing fancy" (Bontekoe 2017: 964). But surely it is not right that our being finite creatures including shortage of resources and time arise only for philosophy and not other disciplines. As Strickland (2018) correctly observes, "if a geography, history or politics department were to offer a similarly narrow syllabus, we would probably think that it was not fit for purpose. The same should be true of philosophy." No other humanities discipline demonstrates this systematic neglect of most of the world's civilizations in its domain as philosophy. In other words, the parochial characteristic of philosophy that we deplore is a problem that other disciplines have recognized and attempted to address in their approach and it important for philosophy to draw important lessons from that. The following observation by Bernasconi (2003: 578) is apposite:

> Just as the study of religion in the West largely ceased during the course of the twentieth century to be a way of promoting Christianity at the expense of non-Western religions, so the study of philosophy in the universities can be redesigned to offer greater opportunity for studying different traditions. Until this happens there will always be a suspicion that, in spite of the pretensions of Western philosophy toward universalism, for the most part Western philosophers will tend to be more provincial in their interests than, for example, many African, Chinese, Indian or Japanese philosophers, who often have mastery of more than one tradition.

In light of the foregoing, and turning our attention back to the question posed at the beginning of this chapter, there can be no doubt that the truly universalistic outlook that we envision for the discipline of philosophy demands change in the manner in which philosophy has been taught and continues to be projected if we are to be true both to philosophy and to humanity. At the very least, it can be agreed that what distinguishes philosophy—that proverbial love for wisdom—is the relentless spirit of inquiry and open mindedness. It is this insatiable quest, this relentless prodding and receptivity and willingness to explore the unfamiliar, that is the true spirit of philosophy. By its very nature, this quest is boundless and inherent to humanity. Any attempt to proscribe this celebration or expression of thinking and reasoning is anathema to the spirit of philosophy *qua* philosophy. When exclusionary tendencies enter the province of philosophy in the form of attempts to foist onto others a parochial view of the enterprise, at that point philosophy becomes paradoxically "self-shackling and self-defeating" (Gordon 2019: 16). The story of philosophy has been itself a theatre of hegemonic exclusions, contrived myths, and distortions that have not served philosophy well, particularly as a discipline that claims to champion critical engagement and to broaden the horizons of human understanding by learning not just about but *from* other cultures of the world. History has seen the development and entrenchment of an exclusionary philosophy which has sought to lay sole claim not only to the activity but also to philosophy as the product of reason (see Ramose 1999, Bernasconi 2003, and Park 2013). For this reason, Bernasconi (1997: 214) is right that philosophy seems to be defined by an uncharacteristic paradox, "the apparent tension between the alleged universality of reason and the fact that its upholders are so intent on localizing its historical instantiation," due to this kind of parochialism. As Strickland (2019) indicates, "it will take a great deal of sustained effort to undo centuries of excluding and marginalizing non-Western philosophies, but there are at least signs that we might finally be on the right path."[4] And so our position moving forward is that philosophers must regard efforts to avoid these exclusionary tendencies as integral to the task of philosophizing, and therefore help to place philosophy once and for all on the path to true universality.

In as much as it should celebrate its successes as a practice, philosophy must also take the time to reflect on its past and to interrogate how that past has shaped, and continues to impact on, the ability of the discipline to manifest in fullness as an enterprise whose universality lies not in the sustained globalization of any one particular cultural tradition but in the cultivation of philosophical expression everywhere. This kind of understanding will serve as a precursor to the goal of enriching dialogue among the world's different traditions of philosophy. One of the crucial tasks at hand for contemporary philosophizing is to give back to philosophy its character of being a creative space in which different cultures can contribute to the growth of knowledge through an interrogation of those priority questions which owe their origin to the existential and socio-cultural circumstances in which the philosopher is located. There is no doubt that for anybody who has considered the history of philosophy over the years, the philosophical tradition which has come to dominate the world has also invariably sought to impoverish it. In other words, the philosophy that has become dominant in our world reflects neither the true spirit of philosophy nor the story of humanity—its ideas, history, or diversity. It is neither representative of philosophical practice itself nor of the multiple voices that define or mirror the different peoples from the world's cultures. It is within this vein that we should begin to appreciate that being true to philosophy constitutes one of the decisive steps by which the journey towards the universal affirmation of the oneness of humanity can be achieved. For that reason, there has to be established a strong connection between rendering the philosophical enterprise truly universal and the celebration of the boundless universality of our oneness as humanity that cannot be severed. Crucial significance must be accorded to the great potential that philosophy as an enterprise steeped quintessentially in the spirit of openness, dialogue, and exchange can achieve for humanity. There is no doubt that philosophy must play its role alongside other intellectual endeavours in contributing to the ultimate goal of increasing, as Sarton (1927) suggests, the amount of beauty, of justice, and of truth in the world as the essential patrimony of humanity. To be able to meet this noble endeavor, it is thus desirable that the study and practice of philosophy be approached interculturally with the distinct aim of learning *about* and *from* other traditions which constitute our living world. The often touted academic mission to promote global and intellectually adept citizens shall be enhanced once we approach philosophy with the open-mindedness that dialogue and cross-cultural conversation demands and in that spirit as "lovers of wisdom follow the beloved wherever it takes us," regardless of the geographical or cultural location (Li-Hsiang 2020: 136). Philosophy as the love of wisdom has never been a preserve of any one segment of human beings nor generation; its existence is evident throughout history and across cultures and will remain so as long as there are thinking minds. Assumptions about life, the nature of self, meaning of existence, ethics, and forms of knowing, including theories of beauty, are prevalent in the world's different cultures and people's minds and these are the bases of philosophy. It is through dialogue *across* cultures that such philosophical knowledge and theories can become part of the worldwide academic practice of philosophy. For that reason we devote our attention in the next section to the importance of dialogue to philosophy.

Dialogue and Philosophy

Once it is recognized that the universal gift of language is the key to the treasures that hold each culture's innermost thoughts, then dialogue becomes paramount. Human beings are dialogical animals and their ability to communicate with others renders manifest the otherwise hidden fruits of their inward contemplation. The particularity of human experiences present the world with a situation where, if we are to make the best out of these multiplicity of experiences, dialogue must become a defining fact of life intellectually and otherwise. The position to be advanced in this chapter is that philosophy is an activity that belongs to human beings and it flourishes irrespective of the cultural, religious, political, racial, gender, or geographical identity of the people articulating it. This diversity represents the true reality of the world to which we all belong. From this multiplicity of existence and experiences it follows therefore, that "those who articulate an unfamiliar philosophy are not, by definition, our opponents or enemies. They simply espouse a different philosophy. To recognise this, is an important step in accepting their philosophical position as an invitation to a dialogue that could deepen and widen our perspectives on mutual understanding" (Ramose 2013: 9). The premise of this dialogue is therefore the recognition and indeed acceptance of the fact that different experiences yield different thoughts and ideas which in turn inspire the various points of departure we take in the construction and formulation of philosophical positions and theses. It is this which inspires every lover of wisdom to pursue, through dialogue, a better understanding of the other cultures that are part of this world. Dialogue, unlike argument, where individuals can speak at cross purposes, assumes prior recognition of our parity as human beings. It is on the basis of such parity that humans can be brought together to grow in understanding through the active process of reciprocal elucidation in search of knowledge and truth about the world (Mungwini 2015: 396). The term "dialogue" has gained significant prominence in contemporary discourse and one element that stands out is its normative dimension, given that in being invoked it presupposes something desirable in terms of the intention, process, and outcome. In the essay "Polemics, Politics and Problematisations," Foucault (1998) emphasizes the characteristically moral dimension of dialogue which distinguishes it from polemics. Once dialogue is taken as "reciprocal elucidation," then the rights of each person are in some sense immanent in the discussion. In dialogue, a whole morality is at stake: one that concerns the search for truth and the relation to the other. Parties engaged in dialogue have to uphold the important parameter of respect for each other. Foucault draws a clear distinction between "dialogue" as reciprocal elucidation in search for truth, and "polemics" where the other is not seen as a partner but "an adversary, an enemy who is wrong, who is harmful, and whose very existence constitutes a threat" (Ibid.: 381). Whereas dialogue recognizes the other as a subject having the right to speak, polemics attempts to abolish the other from any possible dialogue and to declare victory. Of course, even as we laud dialogue it is important to point out that we are not in any way oblivious to some of its problems. For one, it can be used to reinforce "the liberal assumption on the part of the West of an equal field or marketplace where ideas could be exchanged" (Janz 2015: 485), masking the realities of dominance and hegemony. It can also create an impression that harmony and agreement is prized over disagreement. But disagreement can indeed be a source of that productive friction which is beneficial to philosophy itself in terms of generating more questions and therefore more avenues of inquiry. Janz (2015: 481-89) prefers to emphasize the role of dialogue as a "creative tension" and "an engine of conceptual development" which can be particularly productive where different traditions of philosophy come together. Whether one takes dialogue as the beginning of philosophy or as a creative tension that inspires more concepts and ideas, the critical point is that in both ways it is of central importance to the enterprise. At this point, it is important that we briefly turn our attention to the term dialogue itself with reference to its etymology.

> Dialogue comes from the Greek *dialogos*. *Dia* is a preposition that means 'through,' 'between,' 'across,' 'by,' and 'of.' *Dia* does not mean two, as in two separate entities; rather, *dia* suggests a 'passing through' as in diagnosis 'thoroughly' or 'completely.' Logos comes from *legein*, 'to speak'. ... Logos means 'the word,' or more specifically, the 'meaning of the word,' created by 'passing through,' as in the use of language as a symbolic tool and conversation as a medium. ... *logos* may also mean thought as well as speech– thought that is conceived individually or collectively, and/or expressed materially. Consequently, dialogue is a sharing through language as a cultural symbolic tool and conversation as a medium for sharing. The picture or image that this derivation suggests is a 'stream of meaning' flowing among and through us and between us. Etymologically, dialogue connotes a flow of meaning through two or more individuals as a collective, and out of which may emerge new understandings.
>
> Jenlink and Banathy 2005: 5

Of course, if we were to make recourse to other languages and thus try to think through what this concept means in, say, my own Shona language, as one philosopher urges, it would emerge that this is probably one of the activities present in all cultures, flowing naturally from the gift endowed in all human beings, that of language and speech. The experience and reality of being human is subsumed in speech and action and thus in the capacity to dialogue. From the foregoing, we may reiterate the fact that dialogue admits not only to the ability of human beings to use language but also their capacity to reason and to understand. It is this which constitutes the basis upon which meaningful philosophical dialogue can ensue, in the sense of the flow of meaning through two or more individuals as a collective, and out of which may emerge new understandings. As alluded to above, in celebrating dialogue we must always do so cognizant of the crisis of a culture of hegemony and entitlement which has historically refused to admit to our parity as human beings, including recognition of the resultant philosophies as products of thinking. We can never emphasize enough the fact that colonialism yielded to us a world in which suspicions over the ontological parity of human beings continue to mask themselves as innocent philosophical questions concerning this or that particular matter. The reality is that the prejudices regarding the intellectual and cultural superiority of certain peoples over others and their presuppositions are still with us and it is incumbent on philosophers to address this problem at the core of its manifestation, that is, on the epistemic field through genuine dialogue. Genuine philosophical dialogue as Yancy (2013: 99) advises,

> is not a space for one-upmanship, where one's aim is to outdo one's philosophical competitors, leaving them cognitively and affectively devastated and broken under the weight of one's penchant for philosophical jousting and discursive onslaught. Rather, genuine philosophical dialogue involves mutual honesty and respect, though not apotheosis. The aim should be to strive to understand the other and the position of the other (even as one might not agree with the other or the views of the other), to provide constructive criticism, and to share a passion for achieving greater conceptual clarity.

Although we make reference to this point within the context of intercultural dialogue, the weight of this submission carries through even where this dialogue is between philosophers belonging to the same tradition. There is a sense in which this proclivity "to outdo one's philosophical competitors, leaving them cognitively and affectively devastated and broken under the weight of one's penchant for philosophical jousting and discursive onslaught" has impacted negatively on the fecundity of African philosophy and its potential to manifest unfettered and in fullness. Turning our attention back to dialogue among different traditions of philosophy, there is still in existence stereotypes and misconceptions that have a long history and which continue to inspire certain attitudes and patterns of interaction within the province of philosophy particularly when it comes to the so-called philosophies of the periphery. The history of philosophy reminds us not only of the significance that was attached to the label 'philosophy' but also the politics that is apparent in the manner it continues to be deployed. As Bernasconi (2003: 567) rightly points out, "the label 'philosophy' has historically been a name for one of the most noblest activities of the human mind, so that to acknowledge a form of thought as a philosophy is to accord it a status; it is a way of acknowledging the seriousness of that thought." In any attempt to lay the foundation for dialogue, attention must therefore be given to this historical problem and the significance that it still holds for practitioners of philosophy. It is probably the one reason why to this day contestations over the meaning of philosophy including the demarcation of its boundaries continue to predominate the discussions. The notion of boundaries is invoked here to draw attention not only to the existence of different philosophical traditions but also to different orientations even within the same tradition of philosophy. It is this which makes dialogue integral to the art of doing philosophy. There is no question that we would impoverish ourselves if we restrict ourselves to seeking out philosophies that reinforce our own preconceptions about what philosophy should be rather than crossing these boundaries and borders to understand what the others are saying from within the specific context of their own cultures. Those who appreciate the openness that philosophy prides itself in would understand that "philosophy itself is improved epistemically and methodologically with a wide range of perspectives and experiences" (Dryden 2018: 207). And as the African philosopher Wiredu (1996: 144) rightly advocates, "any enlargement of conceptual options is an instrumentality for the enlargement of the human mind everywhere."

In perhaps one of his most influential articles on African philosophy, "African Philosophy: Deconstructive and Reconstructive Challenges," Outlaw (2002: 163) adopts as his point of departure, the distinction between "Philosophy" (with a capital P) and "philosophy" (with a small p)—the former being philosophy as it is practiced in the dominant Western tradition and the later designating philosophy in the sense of "an enterprise more critically self-conscious of its own historicity in ways that inform its practices," being a product of discursive modalities by cultures outside of the Western tradition. The history which has given rise to this situation and the attendant effort to reify the supposed distinctions between the two as eternal rather than purely contrived, constitutes a dogma that we continue to struggle against in the intellectual circles of philosophy. Although the article by Outlaw may not have been addressed to the topic of intercultural dialogue, it is apparent that the dialectic which in part defines the relationship between these two philosophies—that is, the dominant tradition of philosophy versus its counterparts in the periphery—is the reason why dialogue is necessary. In consolidating its own position and credentials as *the* Philosophy, the dominant philosophy has been conscious of the other even as the negative other whose very existence must be denied for reasons most of which, as we now know, had nothing to do with philosophy. Any attempt to theorize on the nature of dialogue between these different philosophical traditions must out of necessity negotiate this history and the asymmetrical relationship it gave rise to, which is maintained to this day. The relationship between Africa and West is a relationship that has been defined historically on the basis of a hegemony buttressed on the logic of negation and invidious comparisons. In a world with the penchant for comparisons Healy (2013: 277) reminds us that "the problem of invidious comparison arises not in virtue of the activity of comparison itself but rather because appeal is made to a standard, such as logico-scientific reasoning, which when used as a yardstick for cross-cultural assessments cannot but fail to show the other culture in an inferior light in point of rationality." It is perhaps this kind of logic which prompted the philosopher Wiredu (1980) to pen his essay with the notable title: "How Not to Compare African Traditional Thought with Western Thought." Where one group takes its own particulars as both eternal and fundamental to what it means to be human, the stage is set for unfair comparison and the subordination of other cultures. This is akin to what Gordon (2014: 89) describes as the imperial significance of standards where one group is made the standard for measuring the other—one group seeks justification while the other is self-justified. It is for this reason that Africans should take seriously the view that the condition that brought about a near obliteration of their contribution to history as a people, as well as the subsequent marginalization of its entire civilization, dictates the terms on which they enter into dialogue with the rest of the world. In the words of Wimmer (2010: 37), "the specific problem of contemporary philosophy arises out of a situation where one of the cultural settings of the past has been more successful than others in establishing itself on a global scale—as being non-traditional but rather as a 'scientific' enterprise." This privileged position, which has translated into a culture of "hegemony and entitlement," is neither immutable nor natural. It is the creation of human beings, one that we can either help to perpetuate or alternatively strive to address through corrective engagement with each other in the sense of encouraging dialogue among the different philosophical traditions in this world. Committing ourselves to this dialogue is the only sure way to address the issues arising from the relation of dominance on one hand and on the other the angry responses that lean more toward polemics than argument, which are in part a direct offshoot of the pain of exclusion and the injustice that continues to characterize the discipline. Despite a history of the apparent unwillingness to share the name philosophy with other traditions of thought from around the world, there is no denying that if it is to be true to itself and to humanity, philosophy has to proceed on the basis of dialogue among the different peoples and philosophical traditions of this world. There are both practical and theoretical reasons why dialogue is important—it holds the promise for a future world philosophy. If we may reiterate the point by Janz (1997: 236), "dialogue between different orientations of philosophy [even within a single tradition such as African philosophy or between different traditions] is not a prelude to philosophy, but it is philosophy itself." In previous chapters I have alluded to the growing number of schools and approaches in African philosophy, all of which indicate the health of the discipline itself. In recent years, we have seen the growth of one such school—the Conversational School of philosophy, with Chimakonam as its leading proponent. Elaborating on the central importance of conversations to philosophy and in advocating what he has termed "conversationalism" in philosophy, Chimakonam (2015: 467) invokes the idea of philosophical space (articulated in Janz 2009), to drive home the point that "the fruits of conversations in different places are not to remain enclosed or enveloped within their places of origin alone," but instead should enter the philosophical space, meaning "an intercultural forum in which various philosophical traditions converge to converse among themselves." In our view, it is this which renders interculturalism not only indispensable, but perhaps the only sure way to engage in the collaborative enterprise of expanding the edifice of philosophical knowledge.

Being an enterprise steeped in human experiences—and therefore in history—philosophy must acknowledge its past and find its way from that past in order to help define the future of humanity. Dialogue with the past, dialogue with each other, and dialogue about future possibilities, and for a better world, are activities that belong to the province of philosophy—it is about engagement with history as it is about the ability to imagine, all which are the hallmarks of philosophy as a practice. In expounding this need for dialogue we do not just take the history of philosophy as our focus, but instead we attempt to look beyond that to the great potential that philosophy holds. We place our hope in the promise that philosophy holds, that is, the great potential it is imbued with, the as-yet-unachieved potential of philosophy (Okere 2003). It is this which brings us to explore the idea of intercultural philosophy to which we now turn.

Intercultural Philosophy

We will take as our point of departure the position that intercultural philosophy is a specific approach and conceptualization of the discipline which takes seriously the view that no single tradition of thought or philosophy can pronounce or consider itself as the only true philosophy for all humanity. Intercultural philosophy therefore premises itself on a particular orientation and attitude, one that "rejects any absolutist or exclusive view from any one philosophical tradition claiming to be in sole possession of one, singular philosophical Truth" (Mall 2014: 70). Within this approach is an unmistakable ethical commitment to the value of pluralism without necessarily undermining the specificity of each of the distinct individual philosophical experiences. The point is thus to try and move away from a situation where one tradition of philosophy is equated with philosophy itself or is taken as philosophy *simpliciter*. Any attempt to equate the general term "philosophy" with *Western* philosophy is not only misleading but also a centrism that is detrimental to the growth of philosophy itself. Of course, where such temptation still persists it would be both epistemically and ethically correct to call that tradition of philosophy by its correct name and not simply refer to it as philosophy as if it is the only philosophy. This is the point of contention in the article by Garfield and Van Norden (2016), when they implore academic philosophers and practitioners within Western universities who teach only Western philosophy to be truthful about what they offer with this telling submission:

Instead, we ask those who sincerely believe that it does make sense to organize our discipline entirely around European and American figures and texts to pursue this agenda with honesty and openness. We therefore suggest that any department that regularly offers courses only on Western philosophy should rename itself "Department of European and American Philosophy." This simple change would make the domain and mission of these departments clear, and would signal their true intellectual commitments to students and colleagues. We see no justification for resisting this minor rebranding … particularly for those who endorse, implicitly or explicitly, this Eurocentric orientation.

It is probably by being compelled to name what they offer correctly and honestly that practitioners of philosophy may be able to appreciate their own complicity in perpetuating that myth which has sought to impoverish the world by foreclosing input from other competing traditions of thought around the world. There has to be a similar recognition that there is a difference between "the history of philosophy" and "the history of Western philosophy"—a conflation of the first with the second is a problem fueled either by sheer arrogance or ignorance. Today, that distinction—as well as a growing exposition of the vacuous logic and politics that sustained it—has become clearer. Arguments for intercultural philosophy and what it envisages for the philosophical field going forward are perspectives that emerge from the realization that the empirical-historical record of philosophy which now constitutes the history of philosophy is itself the product of a radical modification of the proper history of philosophy as it was known. In the words of Mall (2014: 71), "the history of philosophy is not only the history of Western philosophy but also of all traditions of philosophy." The book by Park (2013) among others, alongside the numerous essays by Bernasconi (1995, 1998, 2003) have carefully traced and exposed the underlying reasons and beliefs behind these exclusionary practices of the last centuries in the construction of the history of philosophy. In his book *Africa, Asia, and the History of Philosophy: Racism in the formation of the Philosophical Canon, 1780–1830,* Park (2013) provides penetrating insight into the process of thinking and the underlying reasons behind the effort to reconfigure the history of philosophy. Of course some apologists may try to argue that the conception of the discipline that this history supports was not racist in its design, but the question still must be addressed as to whether it has not *become* racist in its effects. More often, recourse has been made to the history and etymology of the term "philosophy" to infer from there that philosophy is unique to the West since its origins lie in classical Greek culture. And yet as Bernasconi (1995) makes clear, the fact that *philosophia* is a Greek word does not mean that the Greeks were the only people—or even the first—to practice philosophy other than simply pointing to the fact that they knew something about philosophy. They may have known about philosophy at the same time as others practiced it in different locations. In his examination of the various ways in which philosophy could be colonized, prompting proposals on how it could therefore be decolonized, Gordon (2019) draws our attention to the prejudices inherent within the seemingly harmless practice of tracing the etymology of terms to either Greek or Latin often leaving out reference to other languages. According to Gordon (2019: 19), "ending one's investigations into the origins of words repeatedly in Greek and Latin eventually leads to the false presumption ... that thinking began with the birth of those languages." Philosophy is not just European, as presupposed by this otherwise racially tainted ethnic prejudice that hides in the etymology that we often use as part of our historical analysis. The point we wish to make is that there are habits—seemingly harmless but salient—to consider in this quest to promote intercultural philosophy and in laying the ground for a more open future practice of philosophy. Familiarity with the story of philosophy, and in particular the constraints that militate against parameters for dialogue and conceptions of what philosophy is to different peoples from within their own historical circumstances, is important. Respect for truth and openness to the plethora of historical human efforts to make sense of ourselves, and our relationship to each other and to the environment, is indispensable to philosophy. Even in the face of challenges including the skepticism of ultra-denialists, philosophy as a practice must strive to move us closer to the desirable goal of the truth concerning not just our parity, but our ability to contribute to knowledge as the basis upon which to reconfigure broader conceptions of philosophy. Within the context of this history of exclusion, it has been noted that:

> The decision to construe philosophy as a preeminently European or Western enterprise was made in the late eighteenth century. It brought to a close a period of almost one hundred years during which many philosophers in Europe had energetically explored as philosophy or *Weltweisheit* the wisdom of a variety of peoples throughout the world. At the same time, the longstanding belief that the Greeks had learned philosophy from the Egyptians, a belief based on the testimony of the Greeks themselves, was supplanted in favour of a view that philosophy began in Greece. This shift in perspective that amounted to a redefinition of the discipline was quickly adopted in European Universities and it would not be seriously challenged from within the academic mainstream until our own time.
>
> Bernasconi 1995: 240

Clearly, the upshot of all this, as Strickland (2019) properly summarized is that, "from the late 18th century until well into the 20th century, philosophy's past has quite literally been whitewashed. Most non-western philosophies that used to form part of books on philosophy's history have increasingly been excluded outright, while those that remained have often been treated superficially or dismissively, or included only for their value in explaining the development of western ideas."[5] So what we envisage in this chapter is nothing more than the return to openness (in the sense of the spirit) to energetically explore the philosophical thinking of the variety of peoples across the world and to begin to appreciate the significance of the admission that the Greeks may have excelled in their practice of philosophy but were by no means the progenitors of the enterprise; neither was philosophy a unique practice to them as a people. As we all know, the revisionist account of the history of philosophy has yielded a familiar set of works that has come to be celebrated as examplars of greatness, warranting the attention of all who may venture into the subject of philosophy.

However, as Schacht (1993: 431) correctly noted, "the greatest problem with the existence of a philosophical canon is not what it *includes*, but rather what it implies with respect to the things and thinkers it *excludes*" [emphasis original]. The effect of this is clear for those familiar with feminist philosophy and its struggle to reassert the position of women and their contribution in the story of philosophy as it is with all philosophies of the so-called periphery. The canon which now constitutes the history of philosophy has helped to rigidly define what counts as real philosophy and in that respect it has become stultifying by imposing unnecessary handicaps on the discipline. Intercultural philosophy, therefore, cannot proceed without taking the question of the philosophical canon seriously. For with any introduction to the history of philosophy, students are taught not only the story of the origins of philosophy but also what philosophy is. It is important to remind ourselves of the two senses that the phrase "history of philosophy" conveys. In one sense it refers to the academic practice which traces prominent figures in philosophy's past, and on the other it signifies what we may call the story of civilization or simply the development of human thought. As pointed out by Monahan (2019: 9),

> What [is now clear] is that the first sense of the history of philosophy as a subfield of the academic discipline is in fact a rewriting of the second sense of the history of philosophy as the history of human thought. It is a revisionist, or more properly *mythic*, history that erases, disavows, or establishes as somehow exceptional any appearance of 'philosophy' outside of that fundamentally European narrative.

In thus studying the history of philosophy, a clear picture is created in terms of the development or the unfolding of philosophical thought and the canonical figures central to this story where the rest of the world including women have no place or at most appear only as appendages. By drawing from the existing canon which constitutes the history of philosophy, a body of texts contrived through a process that was itself not innocent of politics, the teaching of philosophy today reaffirms and legitimizes this prejudiced and false narrative concerning the origin and development of human thought. As Park (2013: 1) makes clear,

> In the modern university, courses on the history of philosophy introduce students to philosophy as a discipline. History of philosophy courses ... teach students the canon of philosophy in more than one sense of the word *canon*. By recounting philosophy's past (what philosophy was), the history of philosophy teaches what philosophy is (the concept of philosophy). The history of philosophy teaches the goals, rules, and language of proper philosophical reasoning. Teachers of philosophy do not merely recount the history of philosophy, they use it to define philosophy in exact terms and set its epistemic boundaries, differentiating it from other fields of knowledge such as mathematics, natural sciences, social sciences, and theology. Philosophers use the history of philosophy to reaffirm the canon of philosophy in the sense also of the authors and texts that define the discipline and to show philosophy's coherent and progressive development.

There is no doubt that any attempt to change this has to take into consideration not only the content but the mindset of the practitioners of philosophy themselves. But of course, changing a canon is never a simple matter. Although they can indeed be changed, replaced, or reformed, canons have a characteristically inherent conservative nature and to that extent they are imbued with a certain degree of historical inertia. As Ree (2002) observes, although secular canons may not be as rigid as ecclesiastical ones, they are not infinitely flexible either. They "are formed by more or less weighty historical traditions handed down from generation to generation, rather than by any judgements of merit or taste we might choose to make of our own accord.... [Canons] are sustained by a tremendous force of historical inertia" (Ree 2002: 645). And of course, among the forces that add to the inertia is what has been termed "the principle of academic recirculation." According to the observation by Harris (1991: 114), "academics tend to teach what they have been taught, what is easily available in print, what others are writing interestingly about, and what they themselves are writing about; what is easily available in print tends to be what is being taught and written about; what is written about tends to be what one is teaching or others are writing about." Daunting and despairing as this may sound, it is crucial to remember that nothing put in place by mortals is immutable. And as Hein (1993: 565) points out, "from the perspective of those seeking to reform or deform the canon, especially those injured by it, simply gaining control of the instruments of its perpetuation is an important step." The real merit is that armed with this kind of knowledge, it will be easier to understand and thus appreciate that the process of canon reform is not a one-off event but it needs commitment; it will be gradual and at times frustratingly slow. Either way, the important point is that opportunities for change do present themselves now and again, and in any event intercultural philosophy is not an attempt to jettison the existing canon in its entirety. It simply calls for a reconfiguration of the philosophical practice itself and a systematic reworking of the relations between philosophical traditions in accord with the spirit of pluralism. If we are therefore to concentrate on the brighter side, there is a sense in which one can become optimistic that with each additional piece of literature, and with more and more people beginning to take seriously the ideas and thoughts from outside the dominant traditions, it is just a matter of time before an intercultural approach to the articulation and examination of issues and questions in philosophy becomes a contending reality. Of course, it is important to point out that the above submission concerning the problem of academic recirculation—which also points to the amount of historical inertia that characterizes the canon—does not in any way imply that there are no groundbreaking movements in academia or occasional breaks with orthodoxy. Intellectuals are rarely conformists and if philosophers were to take seriously the view of philosophy as an endless quest to get to the truth and put aside mere prejudice, much that is wrong about philosophy could be changed.

In this drawing of lessons from the past and in being optimistic about the future, it would perhaps be appropriate to recall that this history of exclusion and the consequences of which are with us today, is a topic that many feminist philosophers have had to address. Hutton (2019: 686) reminds us that not long ago "a great amnesia had set in regarding women's contribution to philosophy." But today thanks to the amount of dedication and effort from feminist philosophers, it is almost unthinkable to address any topic in philosophy fully without considering the perspectives of women. This story of the attempted "scotomizing of women who have played some part in philosophy's past," to use the words of Ree (2002: 644), and how that has been confronted, provides a lesson to the rest of philosophy. The effort that has been put to change this has not only resulted into notable expansion and enrichment of the philosophical field and its contributors, but it has more importantly, forced a reconsideration of the story of philosophy and with it the teaching canon. The success of feminist philosophers lies in their ability to develop a voice of their own and on terms that rejected being "inserted into a narrative originally constructed without them" (Hutton 2019: 696). They simply refused to be dictated to regarding the set of philosophical questions that they should prioritise, including the research themes and criteria of scientific validity. For them this was a point of principle which we think should infect all philosophies from the so-called periphery including African philosophy. Those familiar with the debate in African philosophy would remember that one of the issues that has remained contentious revolves around the extent to which Western philosophy should be allowed to continue to provide the definition determining what is and what is not philosophy. A growing recognition of the politics around the story of philosophy, including a new appreciation of the fecundity of philosophical expression, is without doubt bringing more people to embrace flexibility in their conceptualization of philosophy in place of a rigid understanding. The same elements which have brought success to women philosophy, such as "openness to genre, to different philosophical idioms, and to other philosophical priorities" (Hutton 2019: 697), can help shape African philosophy and other traditions of philosophy into formidable philosophies defined on the basis of their own history and priority questions. It is understood that the history of philosophy has often obliged philosophy to revise its own practice and we have no reason to suspect that this will not remain true going forward.

Intercultural philosophy is not aimed at overthrowing the existing canon but rather an endeavor to open up the canon and thus enlarge the history of thought in a way that leaves no one "outside" in a world where different cultures and thought traditions continue to thrive in spite of a history that has tried to incinerate other civilizations. As a new orientation in philosophy, intercultural philosophy should herald a new era in philosophy that dispenses with all types of "centrisms," such as the Eurocentrism which has afflicted (and continues to afflict) philosophy. All centrist ways of thinking must be criticized as a matter of necessity, and to serve as the regulative principle for the practice of non-centristic modes of philosophizing. Revisiting Wimmer's formulation of the rule that can drive intercultural philosophy forward may be salutary at this point: "Wherever possible, look for transcultural, overlapping philosophical concepts and theories, since it is probable that well-founded theories have developed in more than one cultural tradition" (Wimmer (2007: 8). Intercultural philosophy therefore has, as its driving force, an appreciation of the different perspectives from which human beings across the world have and continue to make sense of reality including their ability to formulate ideas and theories. It is apparent that this attitude renders philosophy open to dialogue in which no particular philosophical tradition can ever claim to have the last word. Considering that reality is in fact greater than philosophy, what philosophers do today and what they will do in future shall surely continue to evolve, but within that evolution their practice must help to enhance rather than curtail human imagination including the diversity of philosophical opinions. At the heart of intercultural philosophy is a practical and theoretical commitment to openness to engage in dialogue with perspectives of knowing from multiple voices on issues affecting the world.

Multiple Voices in Dialogue[6]

Notwithstanding the different constraints and obstacles that still pervade the philosophical landscape—including of course hegemonic tendencies—what intercultural philosophy seeks is a truly universal dialogue through the restoration at a more concrete level of the multiple voices that constituted our shared humanity before European dominance, and a return to the multiplicity of existence, in full recognition that this is the most promising condition for the future. Clearly, the logic of co-existence demands that we know each other's cultures and learn each other's ways in this increasingly fragile world. This deliberate search and welcoming of other voices (that is, dialogue) is not simply a requirement to meet the demands of intercultural philosophy, but it is commensurate with what it means to be human and with the reality. Through this dialogue, interculturalism in philosophy gestures towards establishing the philosophical practice as fundamentally a conversation of humankind. In its practice, philosophy must identify itself with the values of relationality, complementarity, dynamism, and plurality, and these are by necessity values that are "antithetical to the politics of exclusion and marginalization" a point of concern pursued with vigor within the context of conversational thinking by Chimakonam and Nweke (2018: 295), in their article on the politics against African philosophy. In taking these crucial values as the defining principles of the practice, we are in effect pronouncing on the existential and philosophical reality that the time has now come for philosophy to depart from its past as an instrument in the service of domination and reconstitute itself truly as an enterprise in the service of humanity. It is worth reiterating that as a practice, philosophy must return itself to the principles of historiography which requires that the story of humanity be rewritten through the critical re-examination and assessment of sources and the selection and synthesis of evidence provided by various civilizations into a narrative that can pass the test of credibility. As a discourse that is alive to the demands of its surroundings, philosophy should, like all other disciplines, reinvigorate itself to meet the challenges of its time. Intercultural philosophy opens a unique opportunity within which this can happen. If by philosophy we imply the love of wisdom, which by nature is universal and boundless, then true philosophy cannot avoid crossing boundaries in the genuine spirit of philosophy as a quest for knowledge. With this allusion to the crossing of boundaries, comes the need to remind ourselves of the different borders. Borders "within the discipline, created by different philosophical traditions … borders around the discipline, created by separating philosophy from other realms of inquiry, [and] borders that keep some ideas and people out" (Dryden 2018: 203). In Chapter One, we invoked this idea of borders and boundaries to reflect on the different consequences of these in mapping the terrain of African philosophy. The commitment to this policing of borders by the equivalent of our own philosophy corps or border-force—the excesses of which have impoverished the discipline by, in some instances, rendering it so thin and unconnected to reality to the point of virtual self-annihilation—is one story that has troubled philosophy and which needs no repeating. The borders around philosophy must be porous rather than impervious to the point of promoting solipsistic isolationism. Even as it maintains its identity, philosophy needs to reach across boundaries to other disciplines that can enrich it and at the same time continue its work of enriching other disciplines. Going forward, philosophy has no option but to dismantle those artificial boundaries within itself that preclude others from contributing to the global philosophical discourse and thus continue to impoverish it. By its very nature, philosophy in and of itself is a never-ending discourse (Dubgen and Skupien 2019: 161); it is a continual invitation to dialogue with others and even with oneself. Through these voices in dialogue, intercultural philosophy may be able to contribute towards creating a philosophical practice characterized by a dialectic of schools and approaches that boast an inevitable variegation of insight and ideas on key issues concerning the world at the ontological, social, epistemological, and ethical levels, among others. With the phrase "multiple voices in dialogue," we are here placing emphasis not only on the idea of pluralism in terms of the concepts, narratives, and arguments that can be brought to the table, but more significantly we are talking of dialogue inspired by and drawing from the different conceptualizations of the philosophical endeavor itself. In this coming together, each tradition of thought stands to benefit not only from the inevitable comparative insights that ensue from being in contact, but also from the manner in which this dialectic injects new life into otherwise routinized modes, frameworks, and approaches of doing philosophy. Once it is appreciated that "no living philosophy worthy of the name allows itself to be limited by what philosophy has been in the past" (Bernasconi 2000: 2), then the ground is laid for the continuous process of articulating, negotiating, and revising the task of philosophy. It is when philosophy opens itself to new possibilities that the goal of realizing the cross-fertilization of ideas can be achieved. Writing from the tradition of African philosophy, it is perhaps important that we round up the discussion in this section by drawing on an optimistic note following the bitter historical experiences that Africa and other indigenous peoples of this world have had to endure for centuries. This is something that in part explains why the intercultural approach to philosophy seems to come naturally for many in the so-called periphery in the manner they practice philosophy. No wonder Wiredu (1998a: 147, 152) felt compelled to say the following: "The question of whether philosophy can be intercultural must sound highly redundant to contemporary African academic philosophers.... [because] interculturalism ... is currently almost an involuntary aspect of African academic philosophising. The question is: does it penetrate philosophical thinking in other cultures in anything like the way it does African philosophical thinking?" This observation no doubt applies with equal significance to all other philosophies from the so-called periphery. Whether interculturalism penetrates other cultures in the manner it does in places such as Africa, is an issue that not only speaks to the history of colonial relations, but also to the unwillingness, several years after colonialism, by those in the dominant tradition to look beyond their own tradition. It is a concern which shall remain topical in the study and practice of philosophy for the foreseeable future. What is clear is that while intercultural philosophizing is taking root in certain places within the West, it is yet to become a common mode of philosophizing. The advocacy in support of philosophy in multiple voices arises against a specific historical experience and it is connected to the right to reason. It perhaps follows without much dispute that freedom means a lot to those who have had to lose life and limb to be able to enjoy it, and equally so, the universal right to reason and every culture's inalienable right to intellectual self-determination is appreciated more by those who have had harrowing experiences of epistemic injustice and domination. No doubt, philosophy in multiple voices as a practice is being championed mostly by those who appreciate the significance of the damage caused to the world by denying the rationality of others in history which today continues in the form of the exclusion of others on various grounds and for reasons which have nothing to do with philosophy. The significance of philosophizing with others in the sense of openness to dialogue with other traditions of philosophy as highlighted above, is a trait that seems to come naturally to philosophers operating outside the so-called center such as those in African philosophy. As Wiredu (1998a: 153) makes clear, the assumption which sustains a parochial universalism that all philosophy that matters is Western philosophy is grounded on *a priori* assumptions and not based on a serious study of any non-Western philosophy because "to be based on such a study would be to concede the case for interculturalism in philosophy." So the point is, parochial universalism cannot be sustained on any other grounds other than mere prejudice. To move beyond this prejudice and the apparent philosophical self-sufficiency it engenders is to affirm the point that philosophical insight is not exclusive to a particular race or culture which is the basis of intercultural philosophy. The reception of philosophy as a universal human enterprise is a characteristic cherished predominantly in the periphery and it would transform the world significantly if this same outlook were to spread through the rest of philosophy. Yes, Bernasconi (1997a) is right that the particular experiences of a people can constitute its universal significance. To any well-meaning philosopher, the need to decolonize the mind which stands at the heart of African philosophy, a condition which arises from the non-philosophical—that is, the experience of colonialism—imposes an equal challenge on those in the West to decolonize their own colonial philosophical thought in terms of being able to place it under scrutiny within the context of the wider world of philosophy. That process could perhaps begin from an appreciation of how their tradition of philosophy is critically engaged with from outside, which effectively is the dialectical engagement with other philosophies and thus the very definition of intercultural philosophizing. This is what constitutes dialogue in the face of difference and disagreement: it is not simply another hallmark of philosophy but instead a way to broaden the conversations and to enrich the practice. It may therefore be no exaggeration to say that one of the gifts that the so-called periphery has offered the Western world of philosophy is openness to dialogue (even in the face of some of the most outrageous opinions by some of its canonical figures) and a framework for engaging with philosophy as a universal human enterprise.

Conclusion

We should perhaps conclude by reiterating that unless the current new space race culminates with the discovery of another inhabitable planet, one on which human beings can thrive, there is reason to believe that we are now and for the foreseeable future bound together on Planet Earth. The logic of co-existence demands that we understand and appreciate each other's traditions, including the underlying assumptions that drive our different modes of thinking and being. This is what makes inter-cultural dialogue integral to our existence. It is only through the recognition and acceptance of the meaning, and value of all philosophical traditions across this world, that genuine inter-cultural dialogue, respectful of differences and open to learning from the useful discoveries of other traditions can be realized (Dussel 2013). To be true to both philosophy and humanity, the philosophical practice must transform itself into an arena defined not on the basis of hegemony, but on the basis of multiple voices in dialogue.

Recentering Africa: The Unfinished Promise of Decolonization

Introduction

The history of philosophy as an exclusive and exclusionary practice, and its projection as a European gift to the world, needs no further elaboration serve to emphasize that the consequences of that skewed narrative continue to impact our lives to this day. However, the search for knowledge and truth has never been a preserve of any one particular category of human beings nor generation; its existence is evident throughout history and across cultures, and it will remain so as long as there are minds that continue to cognize (Mungwini 2019a). There is an ongoing struggle for intellectual self-determination that characterizes the practice of philosophy in Africa, including the need to leverage philosophical analyses on the experiences of being African in Africa. In this chapter we turn our attention to the unfinished humanistic project of decolonization with particular attention to the question of "recentering Africa," an attempt to "demarginalize Africa, and to place it firmly at the center of its own history in a world that is henceforth plural; a world whose unity cannot be the result of annexation, or some kind of hegemonic integration, but of periodic re-negotiation" (Hountondji 2002: 141). We frame our examination of this issue within the broader anti-hegemonic struggle for epistemologies from the global South. In this quest to reaffirm African historicity and agency, emancipative struggles such the "Rhodes Must Fall" movement, including questions concerning the canon, will be examined. Being a decolonizing endeavor, recentering Africa is ultimately about the search for a liberating perspective within which to understand ourselves as a people in relationship with the rest of the world.

Recentering Africa

We begin our examination of the question of recentering Africa with a reminder of what Nkrumah has described as one of the major laws of history, namely that "the budding future is *always* stronger than the withering past" (Nkrumah 1965: 252), to express our belief in the potential that the future holds for humanity and in particular those marginalized peoples who continue to fight for political, economic, and intellectual self-determination. In epistemic terms, the struggles that have seen the birth of alternative voices and their continued strengthening around the world is good reason to believe that nothing ever stays the same and that where there is a will there is a way. For those familiar with the story of philosophy, there is growing justification to be optimistic about the future and in particular the ongoing attempts to open up philosophy to multiple voices in dialogue. The above statement, which expresses Nkrumah's unshakeable belief and confidence in the strength of a people to determine their own future even in the face of seemingly insurmountable adversities, should serve as inspiration to the rest of the continent and others in similar circumstances around the world. It is as much a universal truth as a testament to the thinking that has inspired some of the foremost champions of the liberation struggle on the continent. This humanistic struggle remains unfinished and is therefore ongoing. Signs of this are around us everywhere in the world and in recent years the struggle gained worldwide attention under the banners of "Rhodes Must Fall" and its cognate "Black Lives Matter," to name just a few of the numerous worldwide struggles against domination and marginalization. These voices calling for change are to be understood within the context of a history, and that of a world, that has built itself on the basis of exclusion and the denial to others of the universal right to reason. In the context of Africa, the best way to respond to this tragedy is to find ways to recenter Africa, that is, to affirm its historicity, its humanity, and its agency in a world that, while conscious of its past, is destined inevitably to move forward. The history of Africa should serve as the "source in which we should not only see and recognize our own reflection, but from which we should also drink and renew our strength, so as to forge ahead in the caravan of human progress" (Ki-Zerbo 1981: 23). As a form of memory, this history should act as a catalyst for guiding Africa towards the change that it envisages. At the same time, it should serve as an acute reminder of the iniquities of the past and a means with which to avoid repeating the mistakes of yesteryear. For the practice of philosophy this means, with its roots firmly planted in the traditions which constitute the lifeworld of its peoples, African philosophy must develop new and authentic forms of articulation even as it draws crucial theoretical and intellectual resources from other traditions. Being a critical inquiry informed by its own historical realities, philosophy in Africa must define its own priority questions and alongside other philosophies, help set the agenda for a world without hegemony. Ganeri (2016: 168) is correct that "philosophy has been widely hailed, in many historical epochs and many geographical locations, [as] a medicine for the human spirit." It can indeed serve as a cure, when one of the diseases is that of mental colonization; a particular form of servitude both existential and intellectual, that colonialism sought to install as the defining marker of what it means to be African. Credit must go to Africa's own philosopher kings[1] who, from the very onset, positioned African philosophy as not just another meta-philosophical endeavor but as a venture conditioned by explicit commitments to the pursuit of African liberation. In this way, philosophy could contribute to changing society through a systematic exposition of the social, political, economic, and intellectual challenges confronting the continent. The practice of philosophy in Africa requires that we take a closer look at Africa's present condition and reflect on what this means to us in terms of thinking and practical action. If indeed every place has its own story, then we should perhaps follow this up by returning to the significance of the question proposed by Janz (2009: 7): "What is it to do philosophy in this [African] place?" However varied the kind of responses that philosophers may offer to this important question, the need to pay particular attention to the site on which the fundamental tensions of life and thought are played out remains critical. In other words, subsumed in the above question is the attention it draws to what has been described as context-oriented modes of philosophizing. For the African philosopher, there is no question that the practice of philosophy itself is invested with a certain level of moral expectation by virtue of the place within and out of which the activity of philosophizing is undertaken (Mungwini 2020). In other words, history or culture imposes certain types of problems on philosophy, which in turn help define the philosophical practice. As Outlaw (1992) points out, philosophizing is inherently grounded in socially shared practices and not in some transcendental rules with no connection to reality. He expresses a position that is shared by many with his observation that, "African philosophers have generally been much more successful in advancing the enterprise of philosophy, theoretically and practically, as a venture conditioned by explicit commitments and linkages to the histories and historical situations and to the interests of African peoples" (Outlaw (1992: 71). In this vein, the question of what it means to philosophize in an unjust place would follow naturalistically given that, as Serequeberhan (1994: 16) correctly urges, "the proper task of philosophy in Africa is that of systematically elaborating a radical discourse of the contemporary African situation." Part of the mission which drives African philosophy is this concern to fight injustice at different levels and in the modes in which it continues to manifest in the lives of its peoples. Since most of the iniquities confronted by its peoples are a direct consequences of years and years of domination and marginalization, a reversal of this situation would help to place Africa at the center of its own history.

In epistemic terms, recentering Africa should help transform the continent into becoming a center for the production of knowledge. In the words of Hountondji (2002: 140), this entails "constructing a new space of theoretical production, seeing to it that sub-Saharan Africa, today marginal in relation to Europe and the West in the exchange of ideas, becomes fully autonomous, [and] a center in [itself]." There is no doubt that the creation of new spaces for theoretical production and reflection resonates with some of the earlier resolutions of the Second Congress of Black Writers and Artists,[2] who saw it as their sacred mission to liberate their peoples and to unite everyone struggling for the liquidation of colonialism and its consequences, including those fighting for progress and liberty across the world. An extract of their 1959 resolutions on philosophy emphasizes that "for the African philosopher, philosophizing should never mean forcing the African reality through the mould of Western thought patterns. [And that] ... the African philosopher ought to base his/[her] research on the fundamental certainty that the Western form of philosophy is not the only form possible" (reprinted in Okere 1983: 130). Recognition of these key principles would allow the African philosopher the opportunity not only to construct a philosophy that speaks to the realities of his/her own culture, but more importantly bring to the table topics, concepts, and problematics, that would enrich dialogue in their engagement with the other philosophies without capitulating to the already established tradition and its activities. Ultimately, what is advocated through this kind of resolution, as we have pointed out before and following wa Thiong'o (1987: 87), is "the search for a liberating perspective" within which Africa can make sense of itself of course cognisant of other peoples with whom it shares the world. It is crucial to highlight the aspect of relationality which this process underscores given that the project to recenter Africa is not driven by any desire for self-isolation but by openness to dialogue.

In this quest to reposition Africa, priority at the epistemic level should be directed specifically at what Hountondji describes as the problem of extraversion, that is, the practice of being in thought and practice, externally oriented in the sense that everything is designed and oriented to the benefit of the outside world at the expense of the continent. As a system of subordination and ultimately dependency, "extraversion takes many forms including intellectual subordination to the questions and expectations of the learned public in the West" (Hountondji 2002: 232). Just as in the market of material goods, African knowledge was subordinated to the world market of ideas and concepts managed and controlled by outside forces. The answer to extraversion lies in redirecting Africans to make Africa—and not the outside world—the focus of their attention in both theory and practice. Rather than looking to meet obligations of the rest of the world, Africa must seek to meet the obligations of its own peoples. Recentering Africa is therefore an attempt to put a stop to extraversion—be it economic, theoretical, political, cultural, or otherwise—where activities in Africa are organized and subordinated to the needs of the outside world. It is also an attempt to shake off what Zeleza (2007: 2) describes as "the inordinate influence of externally generated models on African scholarship." Although processes and institutions were put in place to subordinate activities in Africa to the requirements dictated by the West, it is worrying that several decades into independence Africans have continued to further arrangements and policies that maintain the continent's dependent position within the global system. The locus of the economic and cultural activities, including research which leads to generation of theory, should ensure that Africa becomes its own center, the point of departure, and, where applicable, the primary beneficiary (Hountondji 2002: 74.) Conscious of its own historicity, Africa must raise its own questions and seek to answer them rather than rely on others to rephrase its own questions and then generate answers to those problems. As Ramose (2000: 53) argues, "the African experience can be and should be the primary source from which to draw concepts to understand and interpret its politics, history, and philosophy." Given the rising interest in what are called epistemologies of the global South, there is reason to believe that things are beginning to change concerning the subordinate role accorded to other knowledge systems outside the Western epistemic tradition. While it may surely be too early to write an epitaph for the West's epistemic hegemony, "it is certainly not inopportune to record the waning of the era of blind faith" (Banuri 2011: 31) to the Western canon. These calls to recenter Africa can be located within the broader decolonial project which aims to divest the continent of the ills and vestiges of the colonial era. Latin American theorists have called this the problem coloniality—that is, the problem of the enduring consequences of colonialism which continue to manifest in the domains of knowledge, power, and social existence. We believe that decolonization should include not only the subversion of such hegemonic systems, but also the legitimation of other systems previously held hostage and whose growth has been severely stunted by the encounter with modernity. Decolonization is "more than merely gaining independence" from the colonizers, but it is more importantly "the process of divesting the African world of all colonial imposition, [and of] undoing imperial domination in all its manifestations" (Eze 2015: 409). Accordingly, the project of recentering Africa is at its core an attempt to achieve authentic liberation for the continent. As a project, it derives from a set of important ontological, epistemological, and ethical considerations. As alluded to in earlier chapters, the ontological consideration is primary. For us, it requires coming to terms with the concrete conditions of being an African in Africa. The key historical ontological requirement is knowing who we are through a critical and hermeneutical elaboration of the contemporary situation. In other words, for a people who have suffered conquest and the subsequent iniquities of history, the ontological concern should revolve around reasserting the meaning of what it means to be African—it is about self-(re)discovery. "Who we are and from where we speak" provides historical grounding to the practice of agency and thus defines, in unequivocal terms, our locus of enunciation.

Since it seeks to right the wrongs of the past, recentering Africa also holds within it an ethical imperative. The objective which drives the quest for recentering is grounded on the ethical conviction that in the world of today "nobody [should] consider his/[her] philosophically or culturally determined rationality absolute to the point that it could function as a universal criterion, in disregard of other forms of rationality" (Bujo 1998: 9). In trying to encourage such an outlook on both humanity and knowledge, recentering Africa constitutes an integral step towards the universal affirmation of our shared humanity as a people. By challenging the foundations of epistemic marginalization, it seeks to create conditions necessary for mutual respect and dialogue across all cultures and knowledge traditions. Recentering Africa is about development, and development is at its core nothing but an effort to sustain and perpetuate human life—its *telos* is without qualification an ethical one. As succinctly put by Bujo (Ibid.: 209), the ethical task of the human person is to identify the enemies of life in order to defeat death. In repositioning Africa, part of the goal is to create conditions that promote human well-being and ultimately to defeat "forces of death" such as poverty, war, ignorance, dependency, and disease.

On the epistemic front, recentering Africa entails engaging epistemic theories from the global South which seek to provide alternative frameworks by questioning the ideology of universalism which has sought to trivialize the contribution of other peoples to knowledge and civilization. To reiterate the point by Wallerstein (1995), universalism is both a faith, as well as an epistemology. Universities across the world have been citadels of this ideology and its propagation. Through their quest to champion so-called universal knowledge, universities in Africa have remained complicit in masking the violence of conquest under the pretext of the pursuit of universal truth, universal ideas and ideals. The decolonization debates in higher education (particularly in Africa) revolve around the paradox of the university as an inherited institution and its role in confronting legacies of imperialism. Being a "gift" of imperialism to its colonial subjects, the ideology of universalism was intimately linked to an exclusionary and historicist vision of modernity where Europe was seen as the model of existence. The universalism born of the European Enlightenment sought to craft a world civilization as an expression of sameness based of course on Europe's particularist experiences (Mamdani 2016: 70). It is this belief in their own role as the vanguard of reason proper which has given rise to the problem that we call today Eurocentrism. Serequeberhan (1997: 142) defines Eurocentrism as the "pervasive bias located in modernity's self-consciousness of itself.... grounded at its core in the metaphysical belief or Idea (*Idee*) that European existence is qualitatively superior to other forms of human life." Universities in Africa have to this day remained some of the faithful propagators of this faith, although we are now witnessing a move away from it in favor of more pluralistic and intercultural considerations. The new point of departure is the now widely accepted position that "conceptions of knowledge, of what it means to know, of what counts as knowledge, and how that knowledge is produced are as diverse as the cosmologies and normative frameworks [that inform them]" (Santos, Nunes, & Meneses, 2007: xxi). There is a growing hunger for a true universalism reflective of the different particulars to which individual cultures can contribute resources in the creation of knowledge. Just as different streams and rivers all flow into the same ocean, so should different cultures and traditions of thought contribute ideas and concepts to global knowledge and forms of understanding (Mungwini 2021). In terms of theoretical frameworks and paradigms, recentering Africa necessarily entails paying particular attention to the theories of Afrocentricity and decoloniality. By placing Africans and the interests of Africa at the core of their approach to problem-solving, these theories inject the agency of Africans into the equation of social and political transformation (Asante 2003), invariably responding to the dictum of the Enlightenment—"*Sapere aude! Have the courage to use your own thinking.*" However, in touting these theories as instruments via Africa can be repositioned, we are in no way oblivious to some of the reservations expressed against them. But our position is that their supposed weaknesses, like anything generated by mortals, are far outweighed by the positives that can be achieved by adopting them as guiding frameworks instead of shunning them. For example, in his article "Europe Upside Down: Fallacies of the New Afrocentrism", a title that in essence summarizes the gist of his misgivings, Appiah (2010) argues that the Afrocentric paradigm and its thesis is essentially reactive and invariably expresses itself as "Eurocentrism turned upside-down". It is in this very nature, he argues, that its weaknesses lie. Appiah (2010: 50) contends,

> It is not surprising, for example, that in choosing to talk about Egypt
> and to ignore the rest of Africa and African history, Afrocentrism
> shares the European prejudice against cultures without writing.
> Eurocentrism, finding there a literate culture and a significant
> architecture, set about claiming that Egypt could not be black.
> Afrocentrism chooses Egypt because Eurocentrism had already made
> a claim on it.

While Appiah makes this very important point on how Afrocentrism is
tinkered with that which it seeks to reject, it is critical not to trivialize
the historical reasons that have shaped such a response and hence gave
birth to a theory which is not only reactive, but more importantly
corrective. By framing itself in that specific mode, Afrocentrism was
conscious that those areas of contestation called for a specific
unequivocal response. In literal terms, it required a combative
response—a blow-for-blow kind of response. Eurocentric claims had to
be dealt with not by skirting the points they raised, but by showing
directly the invalidity of each point. This is probably the point that
Mafeje is making in "Africanity: A Combative Discourse" when he
writes: "we would not proclaim Africanity, if it had not been denied or
degraded; we would not insist on Afrocentrism, if it had not been for
Eurocentric negations" (Mafeje 2000: 31–2). However, in spite of this
historical necessity, we believe Afrocentrism should, and rightly so,
move beyond Egypt as there are undoubtedly other precolonial centers
of civilization south of the Sahara that flourished before colonialism
and therefore bear testimony to the historicity of the African peoples.
And this we believe is what Afrocentricity has now been doing. It is true
today that arguments about the African intellectual heritage and the
ancient civilizations of the continent are no longer restricted to Egypt's
heritage, but also draw on examples from other parts of Africa. On the
other hand, decoloniality is criticized as an antagonistic, essentialist,
fundamentalist, anti-European critique and a misguided intellectual
exercise which invariably places too much significance on the colonial
project. But in so far as coloniality is a fact, and in so far as decoloniality
calls for the end of hegemony through such things as the democratization

of knowledge production and a reengagement of peripheralized knowledges, it holds crucial significance for the quest to build a better world for all humanity. As Ndlovu-Gatsheni (2013: 14) points out, "decoloniality needs to be appreciated as liberatory thought that gestures towards the possibility of another world and knowledge." This is a world in which the imperium of one dominant epistemology gives way and a new world devoid of the epistemic poverty in modernity—arising from what it has excluded from other cultures—emerges and takes root.

As a knowledge project, recentering Africa is inextricably linked to what we would call the 'return' or 'rebirth' of the African knowing subject. We place emphasis on the return of the knowing subject because knowledge thrives where there is a knowing subject. The submission by Alcoff is of utmost significance here.

> If the knowing subject is the point of reference around which all knowledge claims revolve, what happens when the subject has only an indirect and long-distance relationship to its own 'here' and 'now', or when it has an alienated account of its own reality? The result is that it can no longer serve as the reference point for knowledge, or judge the adequacy of claims of justification. It no longer knows.
>
> Alcoff 2007: 86

In Africa, colonialism was, among other things, an instrument for the manufacturing of inferiority to the extent where, metaphorically speaking, one could speak of the "death" of the African knowing subject. Corrective action is therefore required for a new being to emerge, armed with a new mentality. The call for renewed focus on Africa is not a rejection of the West, but rather an attempt to challenge the continued subordination of African ideas to the dominant paradigms and to replace that with dialogue and mutual collaboration. As it took root in Africa, Western epistemology, whether of a religious or scientific nature, was characterized by what Gieryn (1999) calls "a permanent commitment to boundary work." In other words, the practice of Western epistemology in Africa was marked by a "ceaseless policing of borders and a persistent epistemological vigilance, in order to contain and repel the always allegedly imminent assaults of irrationality" (see Santos, Nunes, & Menesis 2007: xxx). What this means is that the rules of "border policing," by which knowledge came to be marked as either legitimate or pseudo, have to be revisited because part of what marginalized the indigenous epistemologies was the "border policing" itself. Silent complicity and capitulation to the so-called universal is inadvertently a celebration of the consequences of this boundary marking. The marginality of the continent is a result of so many factors, including mute acquiescence even on matters that perpetuate misrepresentation of the African knowledge and worldview. For example, through this border policing, anything that could not be explained from the point of view of the Western paradigm was labeled as an instance of pseudo-science. It needed to surpass various levels of appropriate validation until it reached the higher Western standard. The practice of boundary marking also utilized comparison as a tool to measure the acceptability or not of indigenous knowledges into the canon of legitimate knowledge. While measuring and comparing traditions of thought is human and not therefore bad in itself, the problem was the invidious comparisons. In the essay "How Not to Compare African Traditional Thought with Western Thought," Wiredu (1980) draws our attention to this unfortunate tendency, itself commonplace in colonial scholarship of comparing Western science and African folk traditions instead of comparing like for like, that is, Western folk traditions versus African folk traditions. In the words of Wiredu (1980: 39), "instead of seeing the basic non-scientific characteristics of African traditional thought as typifying traditional thought in general, Western anthropologists and others besides have mistakenly tended to take them as defining a peculiarly African way of thinking, with unfortunate effects." In fact, the consequences of this mistake live with us today. There is no doubt that it was precisely practices such as these which played a significant role in manufacturing a sense of inferiority which contributed hugely to "death" of the indigenous knowing subject. It is such invidious comparisons that, in Tempels' (1959: 20) words, are responsible for "having killed 'the man' in the Bantu." But to be able to reverse this, the African requires important tools of liberative thinking. And foremost in the envisioned "rebirth" of the knowing subject should be what Wiredu (1996: 136) calls the need for "conceptual decolonization," by which he refers to a systematic process of divesting Africa of all the undue influences and conceptual distortions traceable to the colonial era that have misrepresented African thinking for years.

The need for conceptual decolonization also places a premium on African languages to be utilized alongside their Western counterparts in providing the tools for intellectual analysis. Although some scholars have raised concerns with the practicality of conceptual decolonization as a project, there seems to be consensus on the fact that such initiatives are important if the conceptual confusions and distortions resulting from the implantation of colonial conceptual structures in the African mind are to be minimized. Wiredu does well to point out through the use of concrete examples, such as his insightful inquiry into the applicability of the concept of religion to African life and thought, why such decolonization is necessary. To illustrate his point, Wiredu begins by observing that according to a certain way of conceptualizing reality which is Christian, "the orders of existence above the human sphere are categorized as supernatural, spiritual, and in some connections transcendent, while the rest is designated as natural, material, and temporal" (Wiredu 2010: 37). However, a careful examination of the categories of thought underpinning this ontological compartmentalization of reality reveals that it is incompatible with the African worldview since for the African it makes little sense to divide the world order into two, calling one "nature" and the other "supernature." The two worlds are ontologically contiguous. In our view, this is what renders conceptual decolonization integral to the intellectual project in Africa. The epistemic reawakening of Africa has to deal with problems resulting from "an internalized conceptual idiom of a metropolitan origin which distorts indigenous thought structures out of all recognition" (Wiredu 1996: 138). The tendency to unconsciously gloss over critical differences in the thinking of our different cultures is not only harmful to Africa, but it is also a disservice to the rest of the world as different categories of understanding reality are never explicated. It is for this reason that in his argument for conceptual decolonization, Wiredu (1996) makes it clear that any contribution which creates new concepts and ideas increases human knowledge in general. Taken in this sense, his position is therefore premised on the need to see the development of other categories of thinking outside the dominant Western tradition. It is at this point that his thinking resonates with those who call for the strengthening of diverse knowledges, including advocates for epistemologies of the global South who draw our attention to the fact that "the understanding of the world is much broader than the Western understanding of the world" (Santos 2014: viii). Since conceptual decolonization calls for serious attention to indigenous languages, the age-old argument for a linguistic renaissance in Africa is thus brought to the fore once again. The point in all this is to demarginalize Africa, and to place it firmly at the center of its own history going forward.

In summary, therefore, recentering Africa means knowledge of Africa, and knowledge by Africans (Hountondji 2009) should be brought to the fore. This calls for what Serequeberhan (2019: 16) describes as the "indigenous reorientation of our philosophic work [meaning a] critically situated speculative, historical, and cultural re-interpretation and interpretive exploration of our neglected indigenous inheritance." African knowledge and its practitioners cannot continue to occupy a subordinate position with regards to knowledge generation and theory formulation. Scientific extraversion—that is, "the feverish importation of paradigms, problematics, and perspectives and the search for legitimation and respectability from the intellectual establishments of the North" (Zeleza 2002: 21)—has to give way to intercultural collaboration. Recentering Africa implies that those who at one time were faced with leaving their indigeneity at the door when entering the academy (Hart 2010) can now work to ensure that their research draws on their indigenous cultures and experiences. This need to recenter Africa and to decolonize knowledge is something that cannot be wished away, and recently it manifested itself across the world in the famous "Rhodes Must Fall" campaign. Addressing this challenge is a debt that we owe both to those who went before us and those who will come after.

"Rhodes Must Fall"[3]

It is true that every generation inherits the legacy—that is, the struggles, successes, and failures—of its forebears. For that reason, one undeniable truth of history is that "we are the fruit of generations past, we are also the fruit of their mistakes, their passions, their errors, and even their crimes" (see Lavabre 2009: 367). This observation is important not just as an expression of the fundamental truth concerning the history of societies, but more crucially as a reminder of every generation's indebtedness to the past and of the obligations this past places on its shoulders to shape the future. In other words, every generation owes it to not only those who came before it, but also those who will come after it, to commit itself to action, for it is only active agents who, in their quest for change, are driven to "act on their passions," and in the process "commit mistakes" or even "crimes." Social reformers, activists, and revolutionaries of all kinds across the world evince the quality of not being afraid to champion what they think is right for humanity. In Africa and elsewhere, most revolutionaries who have worked to bring about change in society belong to this category. It is the paradox of history that most of the visionaries who have changed the course of history were at some point, in the eyes of the establishment and even of those whom they sought to represent, regarded as criminals. This is the challenge of every generation. Our goal is not to agitate or mobilize for some kind of uprising, but to underscore the fact that it is in human agency, particularly one driven by the passion for change in pursuit of fundamental values such as justice, dignity, and equality, as demonstrated by social revolutionaries across the world, that the future of humanity lies. Today such revolutionaries are not limited to politics; they span all significant areas of life, including global climate change, gender, human trafficking, global injustice (whether economic or epistemic), and the rights of the minorities, among others. This is the category within which we situate the recent student protests in South Africa as part of the "Rhodes Must Fall" campaign. For ease of reference, we will restrict the discussion of this issue mainly to South Africa, where the protests were a reminder of the unfinished "historical and humanistic project" of decolonization in the southernmost part of the continent. The idea of the shared debt to the past was itself demonstrated by the multiracial nature of the students who actively participated in the "Rhodes Must Fall" movement. But, of course—and regrettably so—the movement appears to have mutated into other, less desirable forms. At its core was the quest for transformation and the desire to bring an end to the perpetuation of a culture of alienation reminiscent of colonialism several years after independence. Although this campaign had its origins in South Africa, it invariably moved across the Atlantic to England with the Oxford-based chapter of the same name, which identifies as one of its priorities "reforming the Euro-centric curriculum to remedy the highly selective narrative of traditional academia—which frames the West as sole producers of universal knowledge—by integrating subjugated and local epistemologies. This will create a more intellectually rigorous, complete academy."[4] We elected to highlight only this one aim as it has direct relevance to our discussion. The call to dislodge Rhodes both metaphorically and literally (in the case of his statue, which stood at a vantage location on the campus of the University of Cape Town, overlooking his subjects with the omnipresent gaze reminiscent of Bentham's Panopticon) was in part driven by the realization that our condition today as society is defined by our history. To reject the statue of Rhodes is to refuse to live perpetually under the unblinking gaze of the colonial master and all that he stood for. Of course, what the students voiced is not new, for such calls resonate with the history of (South) Africa and indeed of other indigenous peoples across the world. In fact, the famous disagreement between Mahmood Mamdani and the University of Cape Town on the nature of the curriculum offered by the university in its African Studies Program is a good example of earlier expressions of discontent in the new South Africa. We refer here to his 1998 article "Is African Studies at UCT a New Home for Bantu Education?" In summary, Mamdani's argument was that the problem with the course was the result mainly of what the course team *left out*, not of what they included in it. It was about what they did not teach, not about what they did teach. (Relate this to the point we made about the selection of canon earlier.) He went further to characterize the course syllabus as not only substandard, but also poisonous and severely handicapping, particularly for students wrestling with the legacy of racism. The greatest problem with the syllabus, therefore, was what it said to the students not so much through what it taught but what it implied with respect to the issues and thinkers it deliberately and completely ignored. The course was fundamentally flawed because it specifically excluded those debates in the African academy which established the possibility of decolonizing and deracializing the study of Africa. It is exclusions such as these which have reignited calls for the decolonization of knowledge and the academy. We should never forget that decolonization of knowledge is "a call to assume responsibility for the ongoing task of negotiating, contesting, and articulating what [knowledge] is and what it can be. . . . [And] it is for the love of [knowledge] . . . that we must take up the challenge of [its] decolonization" (Monahan 2019: 15). What the "Rhodes Must Fall" movement and the students who championed it have done is to remind society of the urgency of this task and what it means to us as a people. They have helped to keep alive the debate on issues of historical injustice lest these grievances drag on forever, at which point raising them would be dismissed instantly as reckless and reactionary. In fact, what the students were protesting (and rightly so) was the reality that most "independence struggles, though conducted within ideologies of liberation, [have] served to relegitimize and refunctionalize colonial hierarchies and the practices, [and] institutions that sustained them" (Pratt 2008: 463). This problem, the impact of which straddles many domains in our society, is a situation bemoaned by many who see little investment by scholars and opinion leaders even in coming up with alternative political models. The point is made acutely clear by Wiredu (1996: 143) when he states:

> It is equally obvious that Africa has suffered unspeakably from the political legacies of colonialism. Unhappily, she continues in this sphere to suffer, directly or indirectly, from political tutelage of the West. This is due to a variety of causes, frequently not of Africa's own making. But it is impossible not to include in the inventory of causes the apparently willing suspension of belief in African political traditions on the part of many contemporary African leaders of opinion.

It is difficult not to agree with Wiredu, especially concerning the apparent willingness to overlook what could be learnt from Africa's own political traditions and how that could inform the present. But of course, it is also the case that our own political leaders seem to suffer from a northbound gaze which has rendered them unable to move their heads and shift their attention to the local. Mkandawire (2005: 2) was right that "with their ears finely tuned to the voices of foreign experts and deaf to local voices, African [leaders] simply didn't care about local debates, except when they threatened state authority." The disease that afflicts our politics affects everything else. Accordingly, and perhaps sensing the entrenchment of this debilitating attitude across Africa, of failing to imagine other systems and modes of knowledge production and the attendant all-too-happy acceptance of the status quo with little or no reform, students took it upon themselves to draw society's attention to these historical grievances. Through their protest, the students literally dragged the entire system of higher education before the court of reason to defend itself against the charge of why, in spite of its historical mandate, the university has allowed itself to continue to act as the vanguard of a parochial universalism (Mungwini 2021: 112). In other words, instead of transforming itself into the vanguard of the African revolution, the university in Africa appears more than happy to remain an instrument of neocolonialism. When it comes to taking decolonization to its ultimate conclusion and establishing a new epistemic order, the role of African intellectuals cannot be overemphasized. However, in this quest to address the iniquities of the past and thus reposition Africa, our actions and intellectual effort, which in this case must constitute the cure, should not become worse than the disease. It is for this reason that we make recourse to the famous boat metaphor by the philosopher Otto Neurath (1882–1945) on rebuilding a ship that we are already aboard, out at sea, and without the benefit of being able to pull into the dry dock. In this task of decolonizing knowledge, therefore, and to borrow the words of Otto Neurath, "we are like sailors who have to rebuild their ship on the open sea, without ever being able to dismantle it in dry dock and reconstruct it from the best components."[5] Our point is that in this epistemic quest (to recenter Africa and to decolonize knowledge), our predicament as Africans is similar to that of sailors out at sea who need to rebuild their ship. The work has to be done not only without the benefit of certain key equipment, but with the acute realization that if not managed correctly, the task is a perilous one. There is no room for shortcuts or complacence. This challenge, which invariably extends to almost all significant areas of our lives, including economics, politics, and the academy, is one that we must face as academics. The universities and the curriculum as it stands is the ship on which we are all sailing. The ship has to be kept afloat, together and waterproof, even as we renovate it. In other words, our academic integrity and reputation ought to remain guarded. To dismantle the entire ship, to destroy it completely, out at sea in order to begin to build a new one is, as you can imagine, completely out of question. That would be complete and stupid self-immolation. Therefore, the only reasonable option is to proceed astutely and precisely, step by step, plank by plank, part by part, until the rebuilding is complete. It is our considered view that when students and intellectuals call for the decolonization of knowledge, they imply among other things the need to rebuild the ship we are all on. This implies two things: a) canon reconstruction; and b) adopting strategic particularism as the guiding framework or *modus operandi* in our own intellectual engagement and with other knowledge partners across the world (Mungwini 2018: 9–10). We will now proceed to examine each of these below, drawing examples from philosophy.

Canon Reconstruction

> Some philosophers have come to be 'canonised,' and so ranked among the generally acknowledged saints of the discipline, at the conclusion of a process that might be thought of as having begun- in ecclesiastical terms that are not without a certain appropriateness- with their 'veneration,' followed by their 'beatification,' prior to their eventual 'canonisation.' They have gone, one might say, from respect to reverence to exaltation, with the philosophical counterpart of miracles performed in their names having been duly attested.
>
> Schacht 1993: 425

> The greatest problem with the existence of a philosophical canon is not what it *includes,* but rather what it implies with respect to the things and thinkers it *excludes.* This may be carried to the point of overt hostility to anything straying too far from the straight and narrow.
>
> Ibid: 431–2; original emphasis

The two quotations above are carefully selected, not just for what they say about the case in philosophy (which is critically important) but also for their wider applicability to the reality in most disciplines across the academy. As others are figuratively venerated and glorified into sainthood for whatever belief in the value they are deemed to bring to a discipline, the clear message communicated through this act of selection—especially for those left out—is of extreme importance. It is this exclusion and its implications which, more than anything, have been a bane for the so-called periphery, the mental consequences of which it will take many years to undo. For those familiar with the story of philosophy and its unfolding, it has not been unusual that these so-called "saints" and venerated figures of our discipline have also invariably turned out to be much more akin to incarnations of the devil himself for the majority of those who have suffered the consequences of their so-called groundbreaking theories and ideas. The discipline of philosophy has contributed its fair share of such figures, not to mention much of the content that has reconfigured human relations for the worse over the centuries. In this work our effort is directed at highlighting the intellectual significance of re-inscribing the African experience in the academy by focusing briefly on the question of canon. Revisiting this question is a key element within the broader initiative to redefine the epistemic terrain itself, which entails reworking the hegemonic relations between the epistemic traditions. Often used to designate a collection of sacred writings accepted as authoritative because they are believed to be divinely inspired, in secular literature the canon boasts of a similar authoritativeness although it is not derived from any divine inspiration. Like the canon of the scriptures, the secular version has its own cohort of high priests and defenders in the form of various intellectuals and professionals. It is true that universities can propel certain figures and authors into the pantheon of gods in particular disciplines and elevate the mastery of such authors and their works to a sacred ritual. Universities, like temples with devotees, have often demonstrated an unmistakable devotion to specific authors, paradigms, and methodologies despite the expectation that they should be centers of critical inquiry. It is crucial to remember that the establishment of a canon is a task that carries with it crucial ideological presuppositions. It is a process of sifting and rejecting that is itself not innocent of the politics of identity and representation. As communities become more and more pluralistic, disaffection normally arises as those who were marginalized grow to realize that they and their voice are not represented in the canon. As Bruns (1984: 464) makes clear, "a text, after all, is canonical, not in virtue of being final and correct and part of an official library, but because it becomes *binding* upon a group of people." Consequently, to be bound by a text or a set of texts that excludes or distorts the true history of who you are and the contribution of your own people to civilization is to submit to slavery. If what Bruns (1984) states is anything to go by, then it should be anticipated that struggles, contestations, and conflicts over the canon shall remain a defining element of our world until the canon becomes representative and cease to serve as instruments of exclusion and subordination. It is this which gives legitimacy to calls for the decolonization of the canon by those who, for a long time, have found themselves bound by texts that they cannot identify with. It is often said that certain historical moments—such as those associated with political upheavals or revolutions when people are given to patriotism including "the penetration of the academy by enthusiastic movements from without" (Kermode 1979: 82)—seem propitious to canon formation. The movements we have witnessed over recent years, such as "Rhodes Must Fall" and the "Black Lives Matter," are historical moments that undoubtedly create the conditions necessary for the reconfiguration of the canon and for addressing the legacies of the past, including how these continue to dictate approaches to knowledge and teaching. "Rhodes Must Fall" represents an enthusiastic movement for change which has entered our academic spaces calling for justice and openness. For all disciplines, including philosophy, it is an opportunity to pause and reflect on what this opportunity and mood entails for the reconfiguration of the future. In fact, what might seem like attempts to overthrow the current canon are effectively "endeavours to expand it, to enlarge our patrimony and enrich the 'collective memory' that is, communal knowledge and awareness" (Harris 1991: 116). The point we wish to underscore is that regardless of location, universities have a special role in canon construction and revision. Graness (2015) draws our attention to their canon-forming power. Universities around the world possess special influence which they exercise constantly with serious consequences for certain forms of knowledge. They have the power to confer and to withhold credibility or recognition with the resultant effect that some people who deserve to be counted as credible are simply ignored, while others are propeled to the level of gods. Accordingly, "what is considered canonical determines which theories are going to be taught to our students, which concepts and authors will be studied—and which not" (Graness 2015: 88). Every canon by nature "privileges and valorises certain sorts of problems, issues, and procedures to the exclusion of others. And while some exclusions are richly deserved, others may not be. Indeed, some such exclusions may be seriously detrimental to the [specific discipline] and community, as well as to those whose interests are directly affected" (Schacht 1993: 431). By drawing on a selection of theories and concepts and leaving out or openly discrediting others, universities play an enormous role in the construction, elevation, and validation of a particular set of works into a canon. It is in this drawing attention away from forms of knowledge and traditions of thought that are indigenous to Africa that the canon has been unjustifiably exclusionary and the cause of epistemic injustice which remains a major concern for Africa. As the iconography and statues of the representatives of the oppressive era that have been a reminder of the dark chapter in the history of African peoples fall and are consigned to museums, so should the canon which has served a similar purpose for centuries. Of course, in the domain of knowledge the idea is never to get rid of everything but to transform the epistemic landscape, making sure that it is cognizant of the place in which that activity of education is being undertaken. The diversity that is the constant feature of our lives should be reflected in the different voices that speak through the selected canon at any one point. Going forward, it is important for Africans to draw from the canonizing power of universities which follows from their ability to select curricula, as well as niche areas for research and funding in order to reform the canon and help drive the project of decolonizing knowledge in Africa.

Strategic Particularism[6]

The question of the systematic exclusion and occlusion of certain voices in the construction of an epistemic tradition is a story that is synonymous with the history of philosophy as a practice. To put this into proper perspective and refresh our memories, the following submission is apposite: "Of all the intellectual disciplines, none appeared more blatantly and unremittingly sexist than philosophy. From the homo-eroticism of ancient Greece, through the manly virtuousness of

Rome, to the Latinate priestliness of medieval and renaissance universities and the professionalised careerism of the twentieth-century academy, the entire philosophical tradition seemed to function like a male club expressly designed to keep women out" (Ree 2002: 641). While appearance may not always resemble reality, and perhaps the situation long ago may not have been what is often thought, the predominant account of the history of philosophy today gives force to the charge of blatant sexism in philosophy. Other than being "blatantly and unremittingly sexist," philosophy has also been racist and ethnocentric in equal measure. Park has provided a historical account of this malady, including retracing the significant role played by some of Western philosophy's lead figures. We will not rehearse much of what he has stated save to indicate that it is as a result of this conspiracy to keep out women and all the indigenous peoples outside philosophy that we are now party to global efforts to reverse that travesty. As Hutton (2019: 686) correctly acknowledges, "until the late twentieth century a great amnesia had set in regarding women's contribution to philosophy: the fate of women philosophers in history was oblivion. And oblivion is the mother of ignorance." There was a concerted effort to erase not only the record of contribution by women in Western philosophy, but also that of all the other races by an arbitrary proscription of boundaries regarding who is and who is not a rational animal. The apparent unreasonableness is astounding at many levels. It is no wonder that, commenting on what she calls one of the many benefits of reading Park (2013)'s book, Kalmanson (2017: 63) states, "it [the book by Park] has cleared up what remained of my sentimental allegiance to the so-called canon as I have received it. Women from the modern period sit in obscurity only because I am actively helping to obscure them." And this is true at many levels and in many ways; implicitly or otherwise, we have been complicit in sustaining the exclusionary status quo in philosophy. Interestingly, as Zene points out, "it might be worth to recall that the Greek word *Sophia* ... is a feminine noun and, one would assume, less devoted to the more masculine activity of gaining power especially through conquest, violence, and war" (Zene 2015: 24). If what

Zene says is anything to go by, then there is a strong association between wisdom and women which suggests not only that the attempt to erase them from the history of philosophy is totally unreasonable, but even more importantly that the global outlook of philosophy may have turned out differently, including its engagement with the Other, had philosophy not attempted to sever this connection. Today, it is noteworthy that although the situation is far from what it should be, the presence of women in philosophy is improving, but the same cannot be said about the indigenous peoples. It is such exclusionary tendencies— particularly of the formerly colonized—which has prompted calls for the decolonization of not just philosophy, but of knowledge in general. The need to both understand the indigenous thoughts in Africa and carefully study (and therefore reverse) some of the major distortions that have encrusted over the years as a consequence of what Wiredu (1998: 28) bemoans as the "superabundance of characterizations of African thought in terms of inappropriate or, at best, only half-appropriate concepts" requires the adoption of some kind of "strategic particularism." While this concern is raised with particular reference to philosophy, the ubiquity of areas in need of such corrective action, and which call for similar effort, runs across disciplines. This corrective action has to be built from what is already in place at the same time as it seeks to transform the truths concerning our cultures and their contribution to knowledge.

There are potentially two issues that are pre-eminent in this process of decolonization: one, the question of how to do justice to those perspectives and voices that have been systematically silenced and ignored; and two, how to address the numerous distortions and impositions that we have just referred to above. In both cases, the situation imposes an imperative on the African intellectual to place particularistic focus on African knowledges given the neglect they have suffered. It is important to state right from the onset that focus of this nature is not synonymous with isolationism, and neither is it premised on some other blindly vindictive agenda. To become that would be to defeat the whole decolonization project, which is to open up the epistemic terrain to multiple voices and thus enhance dialogue among the different knowledge traditions. As the name suggests and as far as Africa is concerned, strategic particularism arises in response to the history of exclusion and out of the conscious need for self-rediscovery. It tries to render the specificities of Africa's various knowledge traditions visible and to make indigenous knowledges an integral part of the conversation of the present rather than being simply an appendage. Ultimately, the aim is that unlike what obtains now and what was predominantly as a result of the colonial history, the African voice should become audible in any intellectual discourse on the continent. Commitment to Africa, often indicated by the express desire to name centers of knowledge production "African center of X or Y," must translate into an equal commitment to accord voice to the African and with it, the path to intellectual self-determination. It seems on too many occasions the name "African center of X or Y" is deployed for its political correctness and therefore invoked only as another convenient moniker that serves as the seal of approval on knowledge-based activities that do not in any way speak to the problems and concerns arising from the African continent and the needs of its peoples. We insist that there is good reason, in the interest of decolonization, to confront this form of deception in the academy in order to address this challenge of "ethically sanctioned ignorance"[7] as far as knowledge about Africa is concerned. The imperative to re-imagine (and) to reinvent the production, interpretation, and circulation of knowledge about Africa is what decolonization of knowledge is all about. In other words, strategic particularism as an instrument of decolonization is a corrective response to the exclusionary practices so well documented in history, including all these other forms of marginalization and erasure. From the African standpoint, calls for decolonization are premised primarily on the need to correct history and to construct a future knowledge landscape that is democratic. Knowledge about ourselves and its heritage is as crucial as knowledge from others and their heritage articulated on the basis of each of our unique experiences about this shared world. Conceived in that manner, decolonization of knowledge therefore translates into nothing more than the cultivation of two critical intellectual virtues: "one, to be particularistic enough to be capable of knowing ourselves; and two, to be universalistic enough to be capable of knowing others" (Wiredu 2011: 33). If this were to become the new norm in all our intellectual pursuits, exacted with the same intent and spirit across all disciplines, most of the hegemonic tendencies which pervade our academic spaces would naturally wither away. The question of how to do justice to those perspectives and voices that have been deliberately marginalized and silenced should be of utmost concern to intellectuals from across the world. It is this which drive our calls for decolonizing knowledge and ultimately for recentering Africa.

Self-Recovery

As we move to conclude this chapter, we wish to illustrate the intellectual and moral significance of re-inscribing the African experience in the academy with special reference to the teaching of philosophy in (South) Africa. We will draw from the two positions expressed by the philosophers Ramose and Metz respectively. These appear in a special issue of the *South African Journal of Philosophy* published in 2015 under the special issue "Contrasts and Contests About Philosophy." For Ramose, the fundamental problem of philosophy teaching in South Africa is the schism between abstract theory and reality. Philosophy in Africa can overcome this if:

> It takes ethics seriously as the first question of its intellectual investigation . . . Philosophy in South Africa ought to mount an ethical critique of present day South Africa with due regard for 'his-story' . . . 'his-story' shows that there is an ethical exigency for change in South Africa: change that demonstrates not only theoretical but practical commitment to the primacy of the human being – of human well-being—in the constitution of the state.
>
> Ramose 2015: 557

We would extend the significance of this argument to the rest of Africa and indeed other indigenous peoples of the world. Ramose draws attention to the primacy of history and, in particular, that of context in the teaching of philosophy. That this point occupies an important place in his philosophical thinking comes out when we relate what he states above to a position he argued more than two decades ago. In his book *African Philosophy Through Ubuntu*, Ramose (1999: 35) stated:

> For too long the teaching of Western philosophy in Africa was decontextualised precisely because both its inspiration and the questions it attempted to answer were not necessarily based upon the living experiences of being-an-African in Africa. Yet, the Western philosophers that the teaching of philosophy in Africa emulated always drew their questions from the lived experience of their time and place.

Ramose's point of contention is that the teaching of philosophy in Africa has been superficial and it has neglected what is considered integral to its European counterpart—to draw its questions from the lived experience of its time and place. To have a clear understanding of ourselves, Africa needs to be the focus of our philosophical ruminations and the center from which we can interpret our relationship to other civilizations. To do so would be to inaugurate a significant shift in the teaching of philosophy by placing philosophy in the service of humanity, in particular. In his seminal text Wiredu (1980: 16) touches on this fundamental issue of relevance when he argued, "though technicality and a high degree of complexity are inevitable in any serious and sustained philosophical inquiry, the best philosophers are always conscious of the ultimate relevance of their thinking to the practical concerns of life." For our part, the relevance of philosophy to questions of historical justice is paramount. This exigency requires taking seriously "the thesis that epistemic justice is an indispensable complementary to social justice" (Ramose 2015: 557), including recognition that while Africa is in relationship with the West it is not an extension of the West.

In an article entitled "The Politics of Philosophy in Africa: A Conversation," which takes the form of a dialogue with a fellow philosopher, Metz provides a glimpse into why and how he has approached the teaching of philosophy to students in Africa (allow me to quote him at length):

> Rather than ignore African ideas when teaching and thereby giving students the impression that only dead white guys can contribute to philosophical debates, I have worked to put African thinkers and thoughts at the core of my instruction. Rather than to ignore an entire centuries-old philosophical tradition that exists as a living body of thought, I have worked to learn from it and to incorporate promising ideas from it into my research. Rather than patronise African philosophers by simply recounting their views or using 'kid gloves' when evaluating them, I have taken the tradition seriously as philosophy, viz. as a rational thought about fundamental matters, and criticised it where I have found it wanting. Rather than act as though African ideas have nothing to contribute to humanity's development, I have sought to 'export' many of them to a global audience and to put them into dialogue with other philosophical traditions.
>
> Jones and Metz 2015: 540

What we wish to underline from these selected positions is the ethical imperative which goes with the teaching of philosophy in Africa and the importance of history, particularly the African historical reality. This commitment to contributing to African philosophy as a "living body of thought" and the desire to tap into its long tradition of thought, including ideas from its foremost thinkers, is crucial for what it means, especially within the context of our own efforts which seeks ultimately to see a reconfiguration of the philosophical practice and the outlook of philosophy itself. It resonates with the position that we have already examined in previous chapters and belongs together with those international efforts directed at challenging the dominance of a single tradition or single stream of thought in philosophy and the unwillingness to contextualize the practice of philosophy.

While it is almost unthinkable to deny the significance of African philosophy to its peoples and the rest of the world, there still exist other, subtle, forms of academic arrogance "exemplified by disdain, ridicule, and the many varieties of patronizing belittlement, [where] close, careful, and respectful attention given to some thinkers, [is] combined with derision expressed toward others who are different from them" (Schacht 1993: 432). This has been employed effectively and often in order to discourage interest in African indigenous ideas and thinkers. As a result of their fundamentalist attitude, the advocates and defenders of the reigning orthodoxy accept only what they prescribe. They do not take kindly to suggestions that indigenous African ideas can bring something to the philosophical table. Then of course there are those who belong to a group designated by More (2004: 154) as "neutralists," those philosophers who believe that philosophy has to be pursued for its own sake as a second-order activity concerned mainly with the logical analysis and clarification of concepts. And for this group of philosophers, the priority questions of African philosophy stemming from the set of historical grievances that are yet to be addressed at many levels threaten to muddle the proper business of philosophy *qua* philosophy by invoking issues that should be kept at bay if pure professional philosophical rumination is to prevail. Together with More (2004), a similar retracing of these problems in the teaching of philosophy, including the attempt to keep African philosophy at bay and from addressing key concerns such as the problems of race, racism, and systematic exclusion faced by the indigenous peoples, is found in Dladla (2017)'s article entitled "Racism and the Marginality of African Philosophy in Africa." Reference should also be made to the 2016 article by Lamola for the notable title qualifier "Towards an Option for the Excluded," in which he spells out what he envisages as the way forward in transforming the philosophy curriculum in South Africa. Against the backdrop of different existential and cultural-historical experiences of the students, Lamola (2016: 509) recommends that transformation is required in "the *way of doing* philosophy … [philosophy must seek] its reflective-material from the actual experiences and aspiration of people, conscious *a priori* of the marginalised, premised on the quest for justice and good life for all" (original emphasis). The significance of the imperative to change "the way of doing philosophy" cannot be overemphasized. By concentrating on what he refers to as technical aspects of philosophy such as validity, proper names, brains in a vat, justification etc, to satisfy philosophical standards of the global North, Matolino (2020: 1) is right to criticize philosophers in South Africa for having been complicit in fomenting the disaffection and anger that has culminated with legitimate calls for decolonization of knowledge and the curriculum and for their failure to ground philosophy teaching in its African context. The major question is—and to rephrase the point by Flory (2017: 51) into a question— "Why do [most] philosophers continue to see themselves as dealers in abstract, eternal verities expressed in universalistic form and ideas untouched by worldly concerns or the humdrum details of everyday existence like race?" The answer probably lies in the predominant history of philosophy that we are deeply attached to, a contrived one that we have been fed and which favors this kind of bias and idealization. From this contrived history we obtained the concept of what philosophy is, which helps to sustain this attitude. But more importantly this also works well in keeping philosophy from posing at the most fundamental level of reflection those serious questions that could upset the order of existence that philosophy has been deployed to sustain for centuries. There is therefore no better way of ensuring that this order remains in place than to engage the young students in mental games that distract them from the immediate demands of concrete existence. There is little doubt, and here Solomon (2001: 102) is correct, that the apparent obsession with "the philosophical games based on the dubious notion of 'logical possibility' and the continuing insistence on necessary and sufficient conditions, giving rise inevitably to the counterexample contest, . . . [coupled with] the compulsive nature of the games distracts us from confronting the problems that . . . real people face in their lives." This has been the case with the teaching of philosophy in Africa, as the treatment of topics and questions has most often shied away from any connection with historical reality where the philosophical paradox posed by Kantian racism and his moral universalism, for example, never arises as an issue that warrants serious scrutiny. For as Eze (1997: 103) clearly pointed out, all this is allowed to pass because of "the overwhelming desire to see Kant only as a 'pure' philosopher, preoccupied only with 'pure' culture and color-blind philosophical themes in the sanctum sanctorum of the traditions of Western philosophy." Accordingly, as Outlaw (2007: 208) bemoans, abortionists and anti-abortionists' arguments are much more likely to be explored in ethics courses in departments of philosophy than the right to life denied to the indigenous peoples of Africa since the arrival of the explorers and settler-colonists from Europe. From the foregoing, it is apparent that there still exist subtle and other not so subtle ways to ensure not only that philosophy remains barely affected by the real struggles of society but also that modes of approaching the discipline which guarantee the continued reign of the Western canon remain in place.

Perhaps we should also take this time to remind ourselves that almost six decades ago, Nkrumah set out to deal with the politics of knowledge production in Africa through his direct involvement in two key projects namely; the institute of African Studies at the University of Ghana; and the *Encyclopaedia Africana*. Combined with his pan-Africanist vision, Nkrumah sought to use these initiatives to transform both scholarly and public understandings of Africa and to challenge colonial categories about the continent and its peoples locally and globally (Allman 2013). He envisioned forms of knowledge production about Africa that would be "Africa-centred, Africa-based, and globally engaged" (Ibid.; 183), something that would help bring an end to the marginalization of Africans and the African academy, including what Zeleza (2007: 2) called the "inordinate influence of externally generated models on African scholarship." Unfortunately, as Allman (2013: 201) makes clear, the end of Nkrumah's political career had many casualties "but one that has not been fully appreciated is [the fate of] postcolonial knowledge production about Africa." Nkrumah's ambition for Africa to be studied in new, Africa-centered ways, free from all colonial presuppositions, suffered when he was ousted from power. His ideas and vision for the continent including knowledge production were among the unfortunate casualties of the demise of his political career. That said, his projects (had this not happened) could have initiated "a seismic shift in the balance of power in the production of knowledge about Africa" (Allman 2013: 200) and, as Serequeberhan (2009) urges, it is important that we draw valuable lessons from the liberation struggles of our past and in this case from the history of the politics of knowledge production. Perhaps the urgent call to establish "a publication avenue that resonates with the Africanisation agenda" pronounced by Masaka (2017: 442) is a reminder of the need to revisit with considered attention what Nkrumah began in terms of the need to move knowledge production in Africa out of the colonial shadow and its attendant ideologies. Nkrumah was unequivocal about the need to recenter Africa. On the presentation of history, he (1964: 63) argued,

> Our history needs to be written as the history of our society, not as the story of European adventures. African society must be treated as enjoying its own integrity; its history must be a mirror of that society, and the European contact must find its place in this history only as an African experience, even if as a crucial one. That is to say, the European contact needs to be assessed and judged from the point of view of the principles animating African society, and from the point of view of the harmony and progress of this society.

This was the same spirit which animated his vision concerning the *Encyclopaedia Africana* project, in which an independent study of Africa undertaken, as far as possible, by Africans would be a gamechanger for knowledge production on and about the continent. Nkrumah's desire to advance projects that would re-imagine knowledge production about Africa globally and on African terms should be taken up by the entire continent of Africa today. Accordingly, there has to be within the modern practice of philosophy the vigilance and determination to escape the neo-colonial fate (in the sense of the excessive influence of externally generated theory on the study of Africa) and to strive as much as possible to render African philosophy a truly African discourse.

Returning to the submissions by Ramose and Metz discussed above, if we are to tease out the epistemic significance of the arguments of these two well-known philosophers, it emerges in both cases that they converge on the quest for relevance and contextualization of the philosophical practice to the indigenous peoples of Africa. In other words, Africans must recognize themselves in the inferences and conclusions we draw from the theories in our teaching of philosophy. Decolonization of knowledge is about this quest. If we may reiterate, it is about what Ngugi wa Thiong'o (1987: 87) describes as "the search for a liberating perspective within which to see ourselves clearly in relationship to ourselves and to other selves in the universe." The epistemic injustice that the students and most Africans object to stems from "giving students the impression that only dead white guys can contribute to philosophical debates." Therefore, the first "ethical exigency" on this road to epistemic justice should be to dispel this myth by placing "African thinkers and thoughts at the core of instruction," and drawing philosophical resources "from a centuries-old philosophical tradition that exists as a living body of thought" [not a dead one] in Africa; subjecting them to serious scrutiny; and in the process demonstrating their contribution to "humanity's development" (Jones & Metz 2015). It is our hope that in this quest to reposition Africa, and therefore respond to its continued peripheralization, there is much that not only philosophers but other disciplines could take from these submissions. Decolonization, whether of knowledge, power, or being, is at its core an ethical imperative driven by arguably one fundamental objective—"the promotion and sustenance of the well-being of humanity." Recentering Africa calls for African agency, and agency, like the dictum of the Enlightenment, demands that we use our own thinking to bring about the change that we seek. And going forward, and whatever happens, African philosophy will never be the same. It has set itself on the path to growth as an authentic tradition. Philosophy everywhere, including Africa, has its own history. Together with addressing the historical prejudices of the past which continue to impact the discipline, African philosophers must also solidify their philosophy into a formidable practice which speaks to the various experiences and realities of being African in Africa, complete with its own share of competing schools of thought and intellectual communities. We take a closer look at one such school and contending tradition of philosophy in the next chapter.

Conclusion

The question of decolonization and its unfinished mandate in the domains of the economy, politics, and the academy continues to preoccupy us, but what it calls for is African agency. The change that we seek has to be inspired from within, driven of course by the ethical imperative to defeat injustice in the many forms it continues to manifest itself, including epistemic injustice. The strong and seductive lure of universalism continues to pose a threat despite the fact that the world is an ocean of possibilities in which we should happily swim together. The project of recentering Africa requires re-appropriating the spirit reminiscent of the colonial struggles, itself akin to the slogan of the Enlightenment. It requires the courage to act on what we believe but, of course, within the confines of the demands for justice for all. The goal should be "to demarginalize Africa, and to place it firmly at the center of its own history" in this plural world whose unity depends not on annexation, but in the recognition of our varied contributions to this world as one humanity.

Africa and World Philosophies:
The Emerging Realities

Introduction

This chapter focuses on the emerging reality of world philosophies, affirming not just "the embodied nature of philosophy" but also "the diversity of philosophical methodologies, intellectual lineages, and social contexts" (Kirloskar-Steinbach and Kalmanson 2021: 7) as well as the enterprise's groundedness in its own historicity. While philosophy is yet to fully recover from its sordid racist past, the direction it has taken is one that is indeed promising. In this chapter, our effort is to draw attention to the promise that philosophy holds, that is, the yet-to-be-achieved potential in philosophy as a universal human practice. An analogy that compares philosophy to the different rivers and streams that traverse different territories and lands is explored. Philosophy is the reflective and systematic engagement of the philosopher in the reality and problems of his/her time. For that reason, the chapter will consider the specific call on philosophizing within an unjust world, with reference to the emancipative dimension of the philosophical enterprise in Africa. Recourse shall be made to the philosophy of Ubuntu in order to articulate the historical basis of this particular tradition of philosophy which has now shaped into a distinct subfield in African philosophy complete with its own set of priority questions. Our point is that a new era of world philosophies is emerging, stripped of the hegemony of any one particular tradition of thought and within which could be situated all the various systems of making sense of the world and our place within it. Accordingly, we conclude the chapter with a note on the desirability of multiple voices and "streams" in philosophy going forward.

World Philosophies: The Emerging Reality

Philosophy, it can be argued, moves forward not just by celebrating its achievements but also by taking stock of some its gravest mistakes, failures, and omissions. We approach the discussion in this chapter with this particular view in mind. At the risk of restating a position that is already apparent in the chapters covered, one of the gravest concerns for our discipline is how to undo the consequences of a long history of exclusions which have impacted on the growth of philosophy and its celebration as a truly human enterprise. This has remained one of the most serious blights on the enterprise and which continues to impact its practice. It is therefore appropriate that we open this chapter with a brief recourse to some of the conscious efforts undertaken to undo this and to move philosophy beyond the parochialism that has defined not only its history but also its definition as an enterprise. In their introduction to *The Oxford Handbook of Philosophy*, Edelglass and Garfield (2011: 3) reiterate the view on the natural inclination of people "to ask difficult questions about the fundamental nature of reality, about what it is to be human, about what constitutes a good life, about the nature of beauty, and about how we can know any of these things." As such, any reasonably impartial inquiry into the different cultures of this world would find philosophical inquiries of the nature described above widely distributed. In this declaration, it is important that emphasis be drawn to the phrase "any reasonably impartial inquiry," given that where the inquiry is anything but, as has often been the case, all kinds of conclusions can be and have been made concerning the regional and cultural distribution of philosophy as a human activity. Another work that deserves mention is the book *World Philosophies* by Smart (1999), not only for the title itself and what it gestures toward, but also for its significance to the entire project of world philosophies. Particularly noteworthy is the implication of the phraseology of his first chapter, entitled: "The History of the World and Our Philosophical Inheritance" (Smart 199: 1). Setting aside various other submissions that one may indeed find somewhat at odds with the promise carried in both the overall title of book and in this particular title of this first chapter, Smart explicitly declares his commitment "to give a picture of the philosophies of all the world," (Ibid.) and "to remind us all of the plural riches of the human race's reflective heritage" (Ibid.: 10) and in a more pointed way, assist those who have been "too confined in the strait-jacket of a conventional view of the history of the field" to "look with fresh eyes upon the patterns of the world" (Ibid.) and see the many "streams" that constitute world philosophies. The position he takes is indeed premised on the need to recognize that "the varying centres of civilization and culture, together with their outlying peripheral civilizations, have contributed divergent themes to the sum of human thought" (Ibid.: 1). And again and within the same vein, "we need to be conscious of our ancestors of all races, religious and intellectual climates, who have helped to shape human living and human ideas" (Ibid.). References to "the plural riches of the human race" which constitute our "reflective heritage" speak to the very heart of what we have sought to champion not only in this chapter but in the rest of the book. And yet, as a philosopher one cannot help but notice the inadvertent recurrences of that debilitating mode of thinking which is often part of the conventional thinking and opinions about so-called smaller philosophies. We would indeed, and on the contrary, state that there is ample evidence in history to confirm that the dignity of human beings is somehow connected to the putative glories of their ancestors. It is perhaps for this very reason that much effort has been invested to maliciously distort, invent, and rewrite the story of human civilization with the main reason being to inflate the contributions of one group and its heritage to the growth of civilization while silencing and deliberately distorting the input of others. Park's book, *Africa, Asia, and the History of Philosophy: Racism in the Formation of the Philosophical Canon*, is a testimony to this cruel aspect of history, explaining to a larger degree some of the reasons why the world has taken the shape it inhabits today. But of course, this should not destruct from the significance of the journey that Smart defines through his *World Philosophies* and, more importantly, the paradigm it sets out for the rest of us who are keen to follow the wisdom and philosophical ideas that the various traditions of this world make available. Smart (1999) attempts to approach philosophy not on the basis of one dominant tradition and what it upholds, but on the potential desirability of reworking this understanding to accommodate the different facets philosophy has taken and can take in different traditions. As he points out, "we all belong to a crosscultural world, the plural past can be amazingly invigorating. We can exploit several kinds and sources of riches. But the shape of a project of thinking about the world's philosophies depends on what we mean by 'philosophy' and its plural [philosophies]" (Ibid.: 1). What is arguably impossible to miss in this opening chapter is the commendable manner in which he repeatedly drives home the idea of philosophy as our shared patrimony as humanity. His submissions resonate with the position that has always constituted the point of departure in the so-called philosophies of the periphery in their advocacy concerning diversity and openness as far as the question of philosophy and its identity is concerned. In the previous chapters we have, in different ways, attempted to highlight not just the significance of this perspective to our approach, but also for our definition of the philosophical enterprise itself.

Like the individual streams and rivers that traverse the different territories of this world,[1] influenced of course by the geographical terrain and geology of their landscape while and truly incising their own mark by reshaping and reconfiguring the landscapes, philosophies are as much products of their places as they are drivers for change. The different streams and rivers are crucial to the vitality of the territories they traverse. And to allow oneself the chance to drink from each one of them could no doubt constitute the moment that changes not only philosophy but our way of looking at the world. If it so happens that all these streams can drain into some kind of ocean that is the entire world of scholarship without losing their individuality, and from which all of us can benefit, at that point knowledge and philosophy can become the mirror-image and symbol of the boundless universality of our creative potential together as humanity. What will keep the waters flowing, and the disparate philosophical currents strong, is the dialogue and productive friction triggered by this awareness of each other's traditions, which will lead in turn to the creation of more concepts, insights, and (potentially) new theories. Since philosophy constantly asks questions about itself and its own activities, the encounter will inevitably generate more of these questions leading to further creative conversations across cultures and even meditative sessions with oneself. The main problem over the years, however, has been that different philosophies have not been allowed to speak for themselves; even their membership to the broader family of philosophy was dependent on the decision of the single dominant tradition. They had first, if we may borrow the analogy of Janz (2017: 163), "to demonstrate [their] statehood before [being] accorded the privilege of being inducted into the United Nations of Philosophy." But even after this induction they still have to confront the reality of being ostracized from the United Nations of Philosophy's own equivalent of the Security Council in that they are not allowed to fundamentally influence, reshape, reconfigure, transform, or be seen to be tampering with the dominant understanding of philosophy. It is the continued presence of this self-serving oligarchy referred to earlier which poses the greatest challenge to openness and progress in philosophy both institutionally and in written literature. Over the years, the great conversations have been going on, but—as we see at the UN Security Council itself—the dominant philosophy through this oligarchy has been apparently reluctant to loosen its grip on the discipline, causing the pace of change to be agonizingly slow. But if the many voices audible today, not only from outside as has been often the case, but also from those *within* the dominant tradition itself are anything to go by, then a tipping point has arrived. There is a need to build philosophy not on the basis of European preconceptions of what counts as philosophy, but on the recognition of the fecundity of philosophical expression flowing from the innate aspects of each culture and the effort each makes in trying to understand humanity, the world around them, and our place within it. Janz (Ibid.: 157) speaks about what he calls the *"speciation"* of philosophy, a metaphor he deliberately invokes because invariably, philosophy has ecological aspects to it, and the dialogues within philosophy are influenced (in some cases determined) by the borders and paths which exist within and around a place. For those of us working in African philosophy—and indeed this may be true of other philosophies of the periphery—the metaphor should be taken further to speak of what in ecology are known as *"invasive species."* The world philosophies' approach, including calls for the decolonization of philosophy, are in essence a reawakening to the long-term effects of this challenge and attempts to reaffirm and to restore not only the beauty, but also the intellectual benefits, of species diversity. This is the only true option to ensure that vital conversations between the various traditions of philosophy are never to be supplanted by a monologue that would inevitably diminish the riches of our common heritage. In so far as this quest to maintain diversity and thus allow for the different modes of philosophical expression to flourish, there are two ways one might look at the situation of African philosophy. On one hand there is a sense that, and mostly on account of the colonial history and therefore due to our strong connection to the West in more ways than one, our preoccupation with establishing a philosophy that would meet the Western standards in terms of what counts as philosophy may have impeded the growth of our philosophy, and possibly constrained it from manifesting fully on its own terms and unfettered. This is the argument we pursued in Chapter One. It could be said our neo-colonial relationship to the West has also engendered a certain philosophical neo-colonialism that would require concerted effort to undo. But on the other hand, it is also true that African philosophy has carved its own space and distinguished itself as an enterprise that is theoretically and politically conscious of the demands imposed by history and the environment out of which philosophical reflection takes place. Janz (2017: 155–6) captures a perspective that is shared by many within African philosophy when he states that "African philosophy, ... has led the way in taking seriously the places and spaces in which philosophy happens and the constituencies and communities in which it matters. Philosophy in Africa analyses (its) place as an object of inquiry, and also exists in that place in a wide variety of ways." This sense of place contains within it important memories and commitments. For, as Brueggemann (1997: 5) rightfully underscores,

> Place is space which has historical meanings, where some things have happened which are now remembered and which provide continuity and identity across generations. Place is space in which important words have been spoken which have established identity, defined vocation and envisioned destiny. Place is space in which vows have been exchanged, promises have been made, and demands have been issued.... pursuit of space is a decision to enter history with an identifiable people in an identifiable pilgrimage.

Africa is a place with a formidable history of its own and with memories, promises, and unfinished struggles that are continuously replayed, giving to its peoples an identity which inspires and imbues entire discourses, including philosophy. African philosophy, being an intellectual activity undertaken in this space, instantiates both the memories, the struggles, and promises of this place called Africa in this important pilgrimage toward justice and intellectual liberation. A viewpoint to the same effect is expressed by Outlaw (1992) through his widely shared observation that African philosophers, compared to their counterparts, have made significant strides in repositioning their enterprise, theoretically and practically, as a practice defined by its own commitment to the history and interests of African peoples. As its contribution to the world, African philosophy has taken upon itself to question and to contest the manner in which philosophy has been projected and continues to be manipulated as an exclusionary discourse which serves other ulterior goals other than the advancement of human knowledge. Bernasconi (1997a) is right that if Western philosophy open itself up to the critiques of those looking at it from the outside, and learning more about itself it the process, it would be in a much better position not only to appreciate other traditions of philosophy, but more importantly to question some of its own ethnocentric tendencies which have not been very helpful in terms of advancing philosophy as a human enterprise.

The history of African philosophy may be a short one if we insist on its characterization as an academic practice. But "the tradition of

African philosophy, broadly conceived, is almost as old as human civilization, if ancient civilization with its associated mode of thinking is traced to Egypt" (Kwame 2017: 97). In speaking of "Africa and world philosophies" as the title of this chapter suggests, we are referring to African philosophy both as a modern academic enterprise and also to its history—written and unwritten, which includes orature as noted in the chapters before. We take it that the postcolonial practice of philosophy in Africa must also be rooted in the resources that constitute our traditional philosophy. As Gyekye (1987: 11–12) makes clear,

> It is indeed a mistake to maintain that the term 'African philosophy' should be used to cover only the philosophy, that is, the written philosophy, that is being produced by contemporary African philosophers. For philosophy, whether in the sense of a worldview or in the sense of a discipline – that is, in the sense of systematic critical thought about the problems covered in philosophy as worldview – is discoverable in African traditional thought.... Consequently a distinction must be made between traditional African philosophy and modern African philosophy: The latter, to be African, and have a basis in African culture and experience, must have a connection with the former, the traditional.

There is resonance in the way Gyekye accords flexibility to the term philosophy to what we saw earlier with Smith in his *World Philosophies*. There is no need to belabor the point that in Africa, owing to the disruptions of colonialism, "the resources of the oral tradition remain either untapped or only insufficiently tapped" (Wiredu 1996: 134). For that reason, these traditions still retain a contemporary importance that one may not find in other places. It follows therefore that "the agenda for contemporary African philosophy must include the critical and reconstructive treatment of the oral tradition and the exploitation of literary and scientific resources of the modern world in pursuit of a synthesis" (Ibid.: 113). We advanced this position in much more detail in Chapter Two. Given the debates that have ensued in African philosophy, it should not be unexpected that calling "for critical appraisal of our heritage is apt to get on the nerves of some contemporary

African scholars. Yet, our heritage of oral philosophy is, albeit indirectly, the creation of individual philosophic thinkers of our traditional societies, who must themselves have been critical and original" (Ibid.: 150). This is a heritage without which we will find it difficult to remain true to ourselves. And it is this condition which renders particularistic studies of the nature instituted by the late Odera Oruka integral to the reconstruction of philosophy in Africa. If this is not done, future students of African philosophy will not be able to dialogue with their own tradition. The past is integral to our philosophy, as is its postcolonial cousin. Today, the field of African philosophy is a dynamic one, multifaceted and with its own community of industrious scholars. As Hallen (2002: 112) observes, "whether African philosophy involves restoring Africa's links with its ancient intellectual heritage, exploring the nuances of intellectual rationality, or identifying elements of the continent's pre- and postcolonial identity, one thing is clear. African philosophers have reached a consensus that they will no longer be dictated to or tacitly subscribe to non-African standards and paradigms." It is this attitude which will allow African philosophy to stake its own claim within the world's traditions of philosophy. As a tradition, African philosophy brings to the world its own intellectual dimension, its own presuppositions, problematics, priority questions, and orientation. At this point we will turn our attention to one such dimension and orientation within this philosophy, in the form of what has come to be distinguished as the Ubuntu tradition of philosophy.

The Ubuntu Tradition of Philosophy[2]

The concept of Ubuntu features variously in the discourse of African philosophy. And so it may be important to begin with a statement of caution that "like most fundamental concepts, Ubuntu defies a single definition or characterization" (More 2004: 156). Hermeneutics has taught us that "concepts, ideas and philosophies originating from man [the human being] are fundamentally infected by an ineluctable historicity and temporality and are therefore culture-laden and culture-bound and must therefore reflect and bear the imprint of their origins and formation" (Okere (2018: 32). Concepts are unlike other products of nature, such as mountains and seas, in that they have a history linked to a people, a specific language, culture, and place. Therefore, concepts have a "provenance"[3] that connects them to geography and place. That said, we will move between two modes of analysis with regard to our examination of the concept of Ubuntu – first as an ethical concept designating specific modes of acting, including what it means to be human and second, as an indigenous politico-ideological philosophy speaking to the vision of a society. But of course the two are closely connected and, as shall be made clear, arguably they have yielded one very formidable tradition of thought in African philosophy. Any investigation into the philosophical anthropologies that have informed life, including of course resistance to colonial rule as well as the ideological choices made by some of Africa's first crop of leaders following independence, would reveal the centrality of Ubuntu as a tradition in Africa. Most of these leaders in one way or the other appealed to a pre-existing form of African humanism that was indigenous to Africa in their quest to not only rebuild the fabric of their societies following the devastating experiences of colonialism, but also to inspire similar change across the continent. In Ubuntu as an indigenous form of humanism, they saw the foundations of a political and social order that would guarantee the well-being of the African peoples. For as Taiwo (2004: 244) makes clear,

> the ultimate end of any political order is the well-being of its members. One can hardly speak of the well-being of an entity unless one is appraised of what type of being it is and what will best conduce to its being the best of its type that it can be. This is the sense in which some conception, however rough, of human nature is germane to the design and operation of any political order. For, in a sense, no political order can escape some assumptions about what types of humans will occupy or benefit from its arrangements and how the interests of those humans might best be served.

In this search for a political and social order that could guarantee the well-being of their peoples and ensure the best for them, a re-appropriation of the African ethic of Ubuntu as a form of humanism was thus pivotal. It is important to highlight that one of the prolific scholars of Ubuntu that is, Ramose (1999: 51), urges that the concept be rendered correctly as "humanness" and not humanism in order to prevent the proclivity to treat what it captures as somewhat dogmatic and thus immutable. Every organized collective of human beings or society has to operate on the basis of some understanding of human nature including, of course, the meaning and *telos* of existence. This entails getting to grips with what that particular society understands as the nature of the self—a crucial metaphysical question which has remained an enigma of equal concern in terms of its philosophical elusiveness across cultures and traditions. As Okolo (2002: 209) correctly points out, "one of the most persistent problems in philosophy, almost as old as the enterprise itself, is the nature of the self- its status and place in nature." The African ethic of Ubuntu reflects in part the African understanding of the self, its nature, and *telos* of existence. While this is not the main focus of our work at this point, it is important to highlight that exploration of the self as a topic within the field of African philosophy has yielded fascinating discoveries of its own. Not only in terms of the apparent similarities between many ethnic groups across the length and breadth of Africa, but also the range of philosophical puzzles and empirico-philosophical challenges that arise from many of the accounts and which warrant perennial scrutiny. It is one area which continues to fascinate those who choose to pursue the study of African metaphysics.

Let us now examine Ubuntu as a theory of morality. Going forward and where necessary, and for illustrative purposes, we shall appeal to popular sayings in African philosophical literature and others derived from my own Shona culture. However, as Wiredu (1992: 9) makes abundantly clear, "although there are differences of detail and, possibly in some cases, of principle between [one ethnic group's] conceptions and those entertained in other parts of Africa, there are deep affinities of both thought and feeling across the entirety of ethnic Africa." Our appeal to this group should therefore be understood as simply an attempt to provide concrete illustrations of otherwise thoughts that, though expressed in a different language, are inherent in the continent's various cultures. In historical terms, "the culture now classified as 'Shona' originated from Bantu settlements on the high fertile plateau between the Limpopo and Zambezi rivers, bounded in the East by the drop towards the coast and in the West by the Kalahari desert" (Bourdillon 1987: 6). They are the founders of the ancient Great Zimbabwe civilization and builders of the Great Zimbabwe UNESCO world heritage monument. The Shona variant of the concept Ubuntu is *hunhu,* deriving directly from the term *munhu,* which means a human being or simply a person (Mungwini 2017). As an indigenous ethical theory, Ubuntu is rooted in the ineluctable fact of existence and a realization that human beings must assume the responsibility of creating a humane environment within which they exist together. This in essence calls for the harmonization of the needs of the individual with the well-being of the community as a whole. The Shona aphorism *munhu munhu nevanhu* (literally translated "one is only human because of and with others") has many equivalents in the different languages of Africa. Following the rendition of Ramose (1999: 52) this would mean "to be a human be-ing is to affirm one's humanity by recognising the humanity of others and, on that basis, establish humane relations with them." A person is a person through other people, which means the individual's existence is intrinsically linked to that of the community he/she is part of. Social relationships are therefore necessary and not simply contingent. Accordingly, and in the words of Wiredu (1992: 199),

> a human person is essentially the center of a thick set of concentric circles of obligations and responsibilities matched by rights and privileges revolving round levels of relationships irradiating from the consanguinity of household kith and kin, through the 'blood' ties of lineage and clan, to the wider circumference of human familihood based on the common possession of the divine spark.

From the foregoing, it is clear that since the individual is embedded in relationships of this nature, which constitute part of one's identity as a member of the family and of society, to live at all is to live well with others. This in a sense is the normative measure of one's personhood. To be truly human is measured by the acquisition of virtues of character and qualities of personhood that are considered appropriate and capable of contributing to advancing the well-being of the community instead of diminishing it (Mungwini 2017). In order to ensure harmony in the pursuit of individual interests, a set of principles were put in place and often communicated in aphorisms as pithy moral lessons, such as the saying *munhu asina nyadzi haasi munhu* ("one who has no shame cannot truly be a human being"). Therefore, mastery of how one behaves within the society becomes a measure of how much respect one could be accorded as a person. Equally important was the moderation of self-interest in terms of the pursuit of such things as wealth. While everyone was encouraged to work hard, the Shona saying *fuma (mari) haigoni kuti mamuka sei mukoma* ("wealth (money) cannot say: How are you this morning my brother?") was an acute reminder that building human relationships matters more than simply prioritizing the accumulation of ever more wealth. Without retracing each and every moral principle, there existed a host of indigenous regulatory mechanisms, such as taboos and customs, that created a community of self-surveillance and self-monitoring which operated effectively because of the conscious presence of the eyes of the community—a community which included the living-dead as an ever-present reality in the consciousness of the living (Mungwini 2012). The ontology of the invisible beings, in the sense of the belief in the influence of the living-dead in the day-to-day undertakings of the living, provided a metaphysical anchor for certain prescriptions and sanctions on human behavior (Mungwini 2017: 144–50). Once we recognize the special place that sayings and proverbs hold in an oral society—given that philosophy has its special source in the spoken word and thus in the oral—there is literally a mountain of oral resources that we could explore to highlight not only the meaning of personhood, but also to demonstrate the foundations of African morality on the ideas of human and communal well-being. The ethics of Ubuntu revolves primarily around the sociality of human existence and it affirms in a fundamental way the reality that "to live at all is to live well with others"; life is an evolving theatre of coexistence, mutual respect and mutual aid (Wiredu 1992). When Metz (2017: 103), who is himself among some of the philosophers who, through their writings, have put the philosophy of Ubuntu on the international stage, gives the following testimony: "I still remember the shift in my head when I heard an elderly African woman say that for her the biggest problem with being poor is that she has nothing to give away, a view I cannot recall having encountered living in the US," his testimony affirms the point that we are making here about African ethics. In other words, the elderly woman's ability and desire to contribute to the promotion of human welfare, and thus meet her obligations to exhibit humanness to others as a member of society, was imperiled by the situation of her poverty. Thus for the African, the ethical pursuit is not so much about pleasing the Supreme Being as it is about fulfiling one's obligations to others in terms of promoting human well-being. Although of course, when human beings flourish, it is also held that even the Supreme Being will be happy. The point made below is apposite.

> It has often been said that our traditional outlook was intensely humanistic. It seems to me that, as far as the basis of the traditional ethics is concerned, this claim is abundantly justified. Traditional thinking about the foundations of morality is refreshingly non-supernaturalistic. Not that one can find in traditional sources elaborate theories of humanism. But anyone who reflects on our traditional ways of speaking about morality is bound to be struck by the preoccupation with human welfare: What is morally good is what benefits a human being; it is what is decent for man – what brings dignity, respect, contentment, prosperity, joy, to man and his community. And what is morally bad is what brings misery, misfortune, and disgrace.
>
> Wiredu 1980: 6

From our discussion on Ubuntu as an indigenous theory of morality, what we wish to emphasize is that "anyone who reflects on our traditional ways of speaking about morality is bound to be struck by the preoccupation with human welfare: what is morally good is what benefits a human being." If Africa could gain all the technology in the world and still manage to keep this humanistic ethic as part of its culture, as Wiredu opines, that would no doubt make a huge difference not only to ourselves but to the rest of humanity. It is salutary to note that the theme of the 24th World Congress of Philosophy, which took place in Beijing in 2018, was "Learning to be Human," and it was surely selected for a reason. In other words, there is recognition among philosophers as informed members of their respective societies (and of this world) that humanity has drifted ever further from its essence, which is primarily to be human—something that cannot just be synonymous with being a biological entity.

We now turn our attention to Ubuntu as a traditional politico-ideological concept referring to socio-political thought and action. Here we consider Ubuntu in the sense of a tradition of humanism which has long been identified as one of the outstanding features of African culture, a factor that comes across often in the literature, including the above citation from Wiredu. It was for this reason that Samkange and Samkange (1980) propounded "Hunhuism or Ubuntuism: A Zimbabwean indigenous political philosophy" to coincide with Zimbabwe's transition to independence and thus provide guidance to the emerging nation on the basis of a theory that had its roots in African culture. Taken as a socio-political concept, Ubuntu—with its humanistic outlook—proved inspirational in the political philosophies and choices propounded by Africa's first crop of leaders after independence, and it continues to inspire ongoing struggles for social justice with its rootedness in human welfare and the dignity of all people. On this understanding, Ubuntu can be taken as a philosophy of liberation that strives to restore the dignity of the indigenous peoples that has been denied and which continues to be undermined through various acts of domination and marginalization on the world stage. Our interest is to retrace this emancipative dimension of Ubuntu, going back to the ideas of the founders of Africa's liberation struggles, including how that same dimension manifests in current discourses of liberation. This quest for liberation, and to reaffirm the dignity of the indigenous peoples of Africa, was reflected in the political thinking of such postcolonial leaders as Kwame Nkrumah of Ghana, Léopold Senghor of Senegal, Sékou Touré of Guinea, Julius Nyerere of Tanzania, and Kenneth Kaunda of Zambia—a group which Wiredu famously refers to as "Africa's own philosopher kings." These are among Africa's early political leaders who put forward "blueprints of politics and development based on general conceptions of community, polity and the general good" (Wiredu 1996: 145). And, whatever else we might think of them, "these leaders produced genuine philosophies with the most time-honored of motivations [-] that of the critical and explorative engagement of one's own cultural and historic specificity" (Ibid.: 146). They set out to rebuild their societies drawing on the best of what they could find from within their African cultural traditions, chief among which was a brand of African humanism that here we call Ubuntu. This humanism also constituted the foundation upon which the liberation struggles were anchored, as when Nkrumah (1964: 68–9) stated: "Man is regarded in Africa as . . . a being endowed originally with a certain inward dignity, integrity and value. . . . the idea of the original value of man imposes duties . . . upon us. Herein lies the theoretical basis of African communalism. . . . In the traditional African society, no sectional interest could be regarded as supreme. . . . The welfare of the people was supreme." (We implore that the word "man" in this quotation be read as "human being.") It was on the basis of this indigenous humanism, or philosophy of Ubuntu, that Nkrumah went on to propound an indigenous "philosophy and ideology of decolonization and development with particular reference to the African revolution" which he called "Consciencism." Nkrumah was convinced that any ideology to build our societies should be "an ideology which will not abandon the original humanist principles of Africa" (Nkrumah 1964: 70). Even as he drew on Marxist socialism, Nkrumah was of the firm belief that there was a need to recapture from traditional African society "its spirit, for the spirit of communalism is crystallised in its humanism and in its reconciliation of individual advancement with group welfare."[4] In this revolution, Nkrumah argued, our thinking and philosophy must help to restore a community in which each saw his or her well-being in the welfare of the group. While there may be variations in terms of detail, there are indeed generalizable similarities in the expressed drive by the leaders to fashion a new beginning for their countries—and indeed for Africa—on the basis of a political philosophy that celebrated humanness and human dignity. Alongside Nkrumah, we will also briefly take a look at Nyerere. Wiredu (1996) extols Nyerere's theory of Ujamaa (family-hood) socialism as being more intellectually refreshing and better suited to the traditions of Africa than some of the imported varieties of socialism advocated by his counterparts. Shivji (2014: 138), in his article which attempts to outline the building blocks of Nyerere's philosophy and how these were reconstructed and deployed in his policy of Ujamaa, refers us to what we would consider the key premise on which Nyerere proceeded in fashioning a philosophy of reconstruction for his country. Nyerere explained:

> The word 'ujamaa' was chosen for special reasons. First, it is an African word and thus emphasises the Africa-ness of the policies we intend to follow. Second, its literal meaning is 'family-hood', so that it brings to the mind of people the idea of mutual involvement in the family, as we know it. By the use of the word 'ujamaa', therefore, we state that for us socialism involves building on the foundation of our past, and building also to our own design. We are not importing a foreign ideology into Tanzania and trying to smother our distinct social patterns with it.
>
> Nyerere 1968: 2

With this, Nyerere demonstrates that there is nothing natural about being unable to capture the conditions and thinking of Africa using our own African terminology. His approach speaks to the idea of liberation as self-(re)discovery. Crucial in is his approach is the express desire "to build on the foundation of our past and to our own design"; a committed stance on the significance of authentic liberation and self-definition in Africa. In what is described by Shivji as his pragmatic political wisdom, Nyerere was not only fixated on Africa, but his choice of ideology was also a response to the politics of the outside world. What stood out in Nyerere's philosophy were his ideas of human dignity and humanness. *Utu*, the Swahili word for dignity or humanness (again notice the connection with the words Ubuntu and *hunhu*), was inseparable from *usawa* (equality) in the sense that all humans are equal in their dignity (Shivji 2014). Nyerere constructed his philosophy on the basis of equality, dignity, and social justice—*usawa, utu,* and *haki* respectively—cultural concepts that are the building blocks of African humanism. This effort by Nyerere speaks to the liberative agenda that drove thinking in Africa at independence and this mission, which has its roots in African humanism, continues to express itself in the philosophical works of many among us who see African philosophy as ineluctably connected to the unfinished humanistic project of decolonization. The call by Serequeberhan (2009: 47) that those of us involved in African philosophy must be willing to learn from and critically study the concrete practices of various African liberation movements and struggles, is apposite. In these struggles we have the examples of how local philosophies and ideas were used to advance the goals of authentic liberation. The struggles for that liberation at independence were grounded in Africa's specific needs and its local philosophical resources in the form of the traditional values of communalism. As Serequeberhan (2009: 47) urges "in the histories of these struggles we have a concrete treasure house of cultural-historical resources and 'know-how' that has to be critically distilled and appropriated." It is in this light that our interest in Ubuntu as expressive of a heritage that speaks to the concrete and specific lived experiences of being African has to be understood. Having examined the two different (but interconnected) understandings of Ubuntu in the sense of an indigenous moral theory and a politico-ideological concept, we will now explore how these ideas of humanness, human dignity, and social justice have inspired the inauguration of a tradition of philosophy, a subfield within African philosophy, distinct in terms of orientation and with its own priority questions. For this we must give due credit to Africa's "philosopher kings" who saw in our indigenous philosophy, the seeds of African liberation.

Ubuntu Emancipative Philosophy

We shall use the following question as ingress into the exposition of Ubuntu as an emancipative philosophy which has become a tradition of thought in African philosophy, complete with its own grounding assumptions and community of scholars. The question by Biney (2014: 28)—"How can Africans harness humanism [taken here as Ubuntu] towards a genuine emancipatory project in the interests of the dispossessed and poor?"—is (and has been for some time) a central feature of a vibrant brand of African philosophy that has taken root and continues to grow in strength not only within the confines of Southern Africa, but also around the world. This distinct tradition of thought is perhaps largely traceable to the thought of Mogobe Ramose and in particular his seminal text *African Philosophy through Ubuntu*, a book which, according to Kimmerle—one of the foremost proponents of intercultural philosophy—heralds a new approach to African philosophy.[5] By electing to begin his philosophical reflections from an understanding of the history of Africa, its politics, and social reality, mediated through the prism of Ubuntu and from the experiences of the oppressed and marginalized, a different entry point into the construction of a philosophy in Africa was laid out. Hallen (2019: 13)'s characterization of this approach is precise:

> Mogobe Ramose's philosophy is grounded in an ontology of be-ing. That be-ing has attributes which define the being of all of humanity as equal in every important respect. Yet, with regard to Africa and its peoples, that equality has been systematically and inexcusably violated. The task of African philosophy is to counter this in every respect and to work for the liberation of Africa and its peoples.

Drawing from African experiences, from the concrete, from be-ing, from the ethical, and with a clear understanding of the universal oneness of humanity, Mogobe Ramose has helped to lay out a philosophical practice; a specific tradition of philosophy which resonates with the thinking of those who see philosophy as an instrument for change and thus consubstantial with liberation.[6] It is crucial to reemphasize that "the defining ontological unity of humankind, of the human being" has been and remains under assault through all forms of injustice. It is imperative that the practice of philosophy help in reaffirming the humanity of the marginalized. What is perhaps distinctive is the way Ubuntu is taken not only as the foundation, but the mediating concept and theoretical framework with which to build a formidable philosophical practice and tradition that draws on the conceptual resources from within Africa itself and speaks to the problems of the continent's indigenous peoples, not to mention other similarly placed peoples around the world. "Mediating the interpretation by recourse to the original African linguistic expressions where the concept [of Ubuntu] finds its origins and meaning" (Oguejiofor 2019: 121), Ramose has done more than many in explaining the multiple dimensions of the concept and its application to the fundamental problems of society. In elucidating the basis of his approach to African philosophy, Ramose (1999: 49) explains:

> *Ubuntu* is the root of African philosophy. The be-ing of an African in the universe is inseparably anchored upon *ubuntu*. Similarly, the African tree of knowledge stems from Ubuntu with which it is connected indivisibly. *Ubuntu* then is the wellspring flowing with African ontology and epistemology. If these latter are the bases of philosophy, then African philosophy has long been established in and through *ubuntu*. Our point of departure is that *ubuntu* may be seen as the basis of African philosophy. . . . [It] is simultaneously the foundation and the edifice of African philosophy.

Ramose (1999) proceeded to elaborate on the etymology of Ubuntu and its "provenance" in a manner that reveals the essentially intractable manner of philosophical concepts where, in order to fully grasp this concept and what it implies, readers find themselves having to turn to it again and again, and with determination like climbers attempting to scale a particularly difficult rockface (see Ree 2001). It is not unusual that one would find themselves having to answer the call of philosophy by returning repeatedly to those passages at the core of his exposition of the concept of Ubuntu in order to try to grasp the crucial message packed into those few sentences. One such section is perhaps that entitled "The Rheomode: The Philosophical Language of *ubuntu*" (Ramose 1999: 56–59). Here we agree with Ree (2001) that in a subject like philosophy, where intractable enigmas are not rare, the joy of philosophy lies in part in the challenge inherent in attempting to unlock such enigmas and the possibility of arriving at an enlightening interpretation. While Ramose articulates the concept and its "provenance" with specific reference to Africa, he is clear about its universal relevance and applicability to the rest of the world in the sense of a philopraxis, that is, an active engagement in the unfolding history of be-ing-a-human-being in the world.[7] And so Ubuntu philosophy as a tradition of thought offers itself to the world and readily makes itself available as an alternative theoretical resource to be utilized in approaching even problems of universal proportion such as the climate crisis, poverty, terrorism, and social and economic exclusions of all kinds. It is able to bring with it a new grounding and to inspire new questions—as well as the reframing of old ones—on the basis of its principles of wholeness and relationality within the trilogy of existence which includes both the living dead and the yet to be born in our world. This circle of obligation and the attendant mindset it inspires is surely something that the world needs at this point in our fight for survival which the Extinction Rebellion movement[8] (we would argue, and in its own way (love it or hate it) and through their radical activism) has done so well in drawing the attention of the world to. The threat of a looming global ecological catastrophe is a problem which requires, as they would say, all hands on deck. The responsibility to reflect on our being in this world and the challenges that we face as humanity is one that we cannot shirk. Today, it has become very clear that expressions such as "we have declared war on nature," and, "nature is fighting back," are neither hyperbole nor mere figures of speech, as some are wont to believe. In this fighting-back, nature has shown no regard for proportionality nor the precise identity of the culprit and neither should we expect that it will honor any principles of the "just war" theory. This is a sign that

balance needs to be restored in our relationship with nature. As Ramose
(1999: 155) reminds us, "the universe is a complex wholeness involving
the multi-layered and incessant interaction of all entities" and that
includes human beings. Our relationship with each other and with the
environment must be in accord with the principle of wholeness.
Relationality, complementarity, and the pursuit of equilibrium and
harmony within the world of existence are concepts synonymous with
the philosophies of many indigenous peoples from around the world—
it is what defines their relationship with each other and with everything
else around them. Not many would disagree with Kovel (2014: 10) that
we live in an era of both economic and ecological crisis in which "the
dominant system of production [capitalism] appears hell-bent on
destroying the natural foundations of civilization as it thrashes about in
response to economic difficulties." These crises are facets of a much
deeper crisis which Kovel (Ibid) characterizes as "an estrangement from
nature stemming back to the origins of [modern] civilization, which
has now reached global proportions and appears to be on a trajectory
headed toward a Dark Age such as has never been known before, and
one that could even foreshadow our possible extinction as a species."
Nevertheless, time has not yet run out for modern society to draw
valuable lessons from indigenous traditions in order to stop this
estrangement in its tracks. Cultures with different ontological and
metaphysical orientations to those of modernity do have alternative
modes of relating to nature. This is where dialogue across cultures
becomes fundamental. The cultivation of conversations between
philosophies, based on the new culture of understanding which seeks
to transform historical and contemporary monologues into dialogue,
holds the future for this world (Mungwini 2015: 405). Africans entertain
a certain ontological-ethical understanding built on the principle
of relationality which implies recognition and acceptance of
interdependence and peaceful coexistence between earth, plants,
animals, and humans. Emancipative struggles for human dignity and
welfare find their meaning in and alongside struggles for environmental
justice. In fact, from the perspective of wholeness and in accordance

with Ubuntu philosophy, claims to human dignity and welfare are hollow outside a healthy restoration of balance with the environment.

In charting his path for the authentic liberation of Africa as correctly picked out by Kimmerle, and through this approach to philosophy anchored in at least three significant indigenous aphorism, namely, *Motho ke motho ka batho; Feta kgomo o tshware motho; Kgosi ke kgosi ka batho*,[9] [and we would add a fourth one, *Molato ga o bole*,[10] the Shona equivalent of which is "*mhosva haiwori*," literally translated "a crime does not decompose," implying within the Ubuntu understanding of law that "an injustice that endures in the historic memory of the injured is never erased merely because of the passage of time,"[11] Ramose maps out a philosophical practice with roots in the indigenous wisdom of its peoples and one that speaks to the quest for authentic liberation by demanding that the African philosopher abandons the path of mimetic philopraxis, that is, the uncritical imitation and adoption of imposed theoretical frameworks. For Ramose (1999: 36), "the independent review and construction of knowledge in the light of the unfolding African experience is not only a vital goal, but it is also an act of liberation." Accordingly, and in the words of Kimmerle, "African philosophy has to rely on the 'African experience' and not on anybody other's experience, when it strives to express its time in thought. This is an experience of well-functioning precolonial societies, of humiliation and dehumanization by the colonial powers, and of an unfinished process of decolonization and liberation." African philosophy is not an abstract undertaking but requires a philosopher's critical engagement with the reality and problems of the time. Reaffirming its eternal connection to issues of concrete existence, Ramose (2014a: 121) reminds us that Ubuntu is not a philosophical abstraction in the fashion of Plato's theory of Forms, but rather a lived and living philosophy of the Bantu-speaking peoples of Africa. It is a philosophy which speaks to their indigenous past, to their present, and a philosophy with which we shall continue to define the future in this quest for liberation. One can identify the resonance in both argument and thrust with the Latin American philosopher of liberation Enrique Dussel, something to be expected given the existential condition out of which the two proponents philosophize, that is, from the experience of colonialism and marginalization and in search of authentic liberation for their peoples. Elsewhere (Mungwini 2017b: 172–7), we have juxtaposed the ideas of these two thinkers on the concepts of "politics through Ubuntu" from Ramose (1999) and "politics as the will-to-live" in Dussel (2008), in an attempt to focus attention on the existence of theoretical frameworks available in the global South, but with a universal applicability that can transform the dominant practice of politics in this world and indeed our relations as humanity. Dussel (2008) identifies the "will-to-live" as the "originary tendency of all human beings." The "will-to-live" is therefore not just that of the individual subject, but that of the entire community; it has to do with the sense of belonging and taking responsibility. It is the "will-to-live" not just as an individual but together. To belong to a particular community entails taking care of the problems it faces, including poverty, disease, and other forces like climate change that threaten human existence. In this way, Dussel places primacy on human life in the practice of politics. Likewise, Ramose (1999) premises his discussion of "politics through *ubuntu*" on the famous African aphorism which states that "to be human is to affirm one's humanness by recognising the same in others and, on that basis, establish humane relations with them." According to Ramose, the value of this aphorism derives from two very significant interrelated philosophical principles; first that "the individual human being is an object of intrinsic value in its own right"— if this were not the case, it would be senseless to base the affirmation of one's humanness on the recognition of the same in the other; and second, "a human being is truly human only in the context of actual relations with other beings" (Ramose 1999: 138). To affirm the existence of the other is an ontological necessity for our own existence as human beings. This speaks to the significance of relationality within the African existential framework, including the ideas of oneness (the ontological unity of the human family) and openness to the other. Our brief juxtaposition of the ideas from these two authors reveals not just similar preoccupations in the two traditions of philosophy, but also affirms that crucial oneness of humanity in the sense of our shared desire for dignity.

The Ubuntu tradition of African philosophy has positioned itself at the center of the struggle for justice and self-determination and by that jettisoning—and rightly so—the otherwise sterile pursuit of the abstract. There is an inherent emancipatory urge that is, therefore, historical and which has conferred to African philosophy its identity as a uniquely context-oriented tradition. Even as it seeks to satisfy the quest for knowledge, this brand of African philosophy proceeds on the realization that philosophy cannot hide behind the abstract quest for knowledge at the expense of its practical and ethical commitments (Mungwini 2020: 1–2). Perhaps it should not come as a surprise, therefore, that ever more people in African universities and across society are waking up to the need to ground themselves in the indigenous philosophical foundations and, in particular, in the conceptual weapons at its disposal which invariably provide them with more ammunition to deal with their own discipline-specific issues. Not long ago, the intellectual landscape in South Africa witnessed widespread discontent directed at the enduring legacies of colonialism on the epistemic field, which came to be epitomized in the "Rhodes Must Fall" movement. This decolonizing endeavor, which is of course grounded on a particular philosophical mode of thought and action (one inspired by the restoration of dignity), traces its roots to the humanistic struggles for liberation. Today, this emancipative quest—which has become the defining character of a brand of philosophy that inspires calls for the decolonization of knowledge and the academy—owes its origins to the historical synergy between Ubuntu and the struggle for liberation. This synergy has been brought into sharp focus by a growing subfield within contemporary African philosophy which takes as its point of departure, explicit commitment to questions of historical justice and dignity for all. African philosophy, as Ramose (1999: iv) proclaims, "contains an ineliminable liberative dimension," and it can be that only "when it takes ethics seriously as the first question of its intellectual investigation" (Ramose 2015: 557). We have traced the history of a specific tradition of philosophy which, drawing its inspiration from the indigenous ethico-political ideals of Ubuntu, proposes its own approach and sets of questions to the practice of philosophy. Grounded in an ontology of be-ing, it gestures to the world the need to ground philosophical practice on the universal ontological oneness of humanity, and on that basis restore to philosophy and to our beloved discipline that richness and diversity, which can be amazingly reinvigorating. We are convinced that within the ambit of the world philosophies approach, there is reason to be optimistic that the time has now come for us all to work to reconfigure the practice and to exploit all the different kinds of resources and riches at our disposal with an openness that is the defining feature of philosophy.

Different Streams—Multiple Voices

In our philosophical discourses and discussions, we must allow non-Western traditions to contribute not just new concepts, thesis, narratives, descriptions, and arguments, but also new conceptions of the philosophical endeavour itself ... [F]rom the ancient Greeks to twentieth century philosophers ... the very definition of philosophy has been almost incessantly disputed and transformed. Why should not other, non-Western voices be allowed into this dialogue and debate? To be sure, they may challenge previous definitions in ways unimagined. So much the better. 'Let a hundred flowers blossom and a hundred schools of thought contend,' and let no one, ... not any of our department chairs, impose from above an orthodoxy on this dialogue about what it means to practice philosophy.

                                                           Davis 2017a: 124–5

We begin this section with a submission that affirms what might be described as the major contention of this entire work. Yes, it would be fine for other traditions of philosophy to contribute to the stock of concepts, arguments, and narratives apart from those propounded by the dominant philosophy, but that on its own is not enough. We agree with Davis: "let this dialogue be about what it means to practice philosophy." The possibility is there that the input like that of Ubuntu tradition, discussed above, may help to transform the practice itself in unimaginable ways. Philosophy must measure up to what it promises— the freedom to think and to imagine without any mental shackles. The manner in which philosophy is practiced places shackles on other traditions; it is also self-shackling in the way it has been conceived. It is perhaps for this very reason (although there are others) that Gordon (2019) argues that philosophy is in need of decolonization. There is a sense in which it has to be saved from itself. The call by Davis to "let a hundred flowers blossom and a hundred schools of thought contend," not only resonates with our thinking, but it is the crux of a long-running and ongoing struggle that has defined the work and life of so many philosophers from around the world. For Ganeri (2016: 136), a new age is emerging in philosophy, one marked by a rising appreciation of the value of world philosophies, increased internationalization of the student body, and philosophical pluralism, including commitments to diversify not only the curriculum but also its practitioners. The latter is what Kirloskar-Steinbach (2019) calls practitioner diversity and the former, content diversity. There is growing recognition of not only the different sources of philosophy, but also of the immanent potential and possibilities about the worldliness of philosophy. As the introduction by Smart (1999) discussed above indicates, philosophy can take different forms and it is important that our conceptualization of philosophy takes in that variety, including the multimedia through which philosophical ideas are expressed in different cultures. Progress towards a richer and more complex understanding of philosophy—one that recognizes the fecundity of philosophical expression—is in keeping not only with our diversity as thinkers, but also with the diversity of our cultures as the material resources from which philosophy is nourished. For once, we should be able to rise above what Bernasconi (2000: 5) describes as the "the restrictive definition of philosophy that has tended to operate in universities for various institutional and political reasons." It is only in this way that we can indeed begin to engage seriously, now and in the future, with the collective intellectual riches bequeathed to us. Philosophy must no longer be equated simply with what we have inherited from the dominant tradition and its designation of what philosophy should be. Rather, our approach to philosophy must be open and it must include not just the prominent figures and their views but also—and more importantly—"our sense of what it means to *do* philosophy" (Monahan 2019: 13), within the context of our African space. We are often reminded that the world is much broader than any one perspective can offer, implying even more significantly for our purpose here that reality is greater than philosophy. It is this message which the world philosophies approach makes not only apparent, but the foundation upon which to engage with each other and other traditions of philosophy in the world. We reiterate the position by Ramose (2014: 73) that, "no one ... has a prior, superior and exclusive right to define the meaning and function of philosophy on behalf of the whole of humanity." Here we wish to return to our analogy of philosophy being like different streams and rivers. The different streams and multiple voices are visible and audible only when the history of philosophy ceases to be taken as synonymous with the story of *Western* philosophy, and instead designates the development of human thought in general. There has been, as highlighted earlier in the book, a systematic and very evident pattern of exclusion in philosophy whereby "philosophical traditions of historically *colonizing* peoples are understood to be philosophy *as such*, while traditions of thought among the *colonized* are at best marginal and more commonly ignored altogether" (Monahan 2019: 9) [original emphasis]. To be able to bring an end to this situation, and therefore deal with the many ways in which the dominant view of philosophy has been constraining in terms of constricting the cultural spaces within which philosophy can flourish, philosophers today must take it as their business to liberate philosophy in the sense of decolonizing its practice. As Monahan (2019) argues, we must assume responsibility for negotiating, contesting, and articulating what philosophy is and what it can be. We must continue to reconfigure the practice and to fashion ideas and theories in response to our own time and place, as was the case with all great thinkers of yesteryear. We should do this with the ultimate aim of bringing forth new conceptions of the philosophical endeavor itself.

That today we speak of "world philosophies" is indeed testimony to the growing realization of the diversity of philosophical orientations, approaches, and assumptions. It is a reminder that the agenda of philosophy is not cast in stone and neither are the approaches for doing it. The philosophical terrain from time to time is a landscape whose boundaries are continuously up for renegotiation with, in some cases, what previously counted as philosophy being discarded and new candidates being admitted. Philosophical practice, even within a single tradition, is inherently plural and the "gift of wisdom" can no longer be conceived as the exclusive preserve of any one particular tradition, as Zene (2015: 28) makes clear. Today, and speaking only about Africa, in terms of the distribution and dissemination of scholarly ideas, there are marked changes at the international level and if what Metz (2018: 210) says is anything to go by, "the African tradition of moral and political philosophy [now features] routinely in books and journals with global reach [and] it is not unusual these days to find African ethical perspectives in internationally influential textbooks, anthologies and collective volumes." Although much still needs to be done in the other traditional branches of philosophy, it does point to the fact that global interest in African philosophy is steadily gaining momentum. The world philosophies approach introduces a future that is open and one that tries to move beyond the presuppositions that have affected the contribution of other traditions of thought to the enterprise. Once we are able to approach the different traditions of philosophy as streams and rivers within which we can swim—implying acquaintance and active involvement with other traditions of thought—new creative spaces emerge alongside new concepts and theories. The various streams in their own represent the growing presence of multiple voices on the philosophical platform. In this multiplicity of voices, ever more creative conversations about our experiences of the world will ensue and with them, new questions and insights about reality.

The future of philosophy and its vitality depends on the successful restoration to philosophy of its worldliness as a practice that is not only diverse but constantly evolving in response to its own time. World philosophies restores the richness that belongs to philosophy and, after all, as one famous African philosopher declared, any enlargement of the conceptual field is an enlargement of human minds everywhere. Perhaps significant in these developments is the fact that philosophy seems to be moving ever closer to resembling something of the conversation of humankind and this, in part, because other traditions of the world, "locally grounded in lived experience and reflection upon it, are finding new autonomous and authentic forms of articulation" (Ganeri 2016: 137). This development should help to release the enterprise from the centuries-old asphyxiating monotony of mimetic philopraxis. It is clear that we cannot play down the diversity of philosophy without undermining the enterprise in ways that are detrimental to the growth of our knowledge about the world. It is within the world philosophies approach that the promise of reclaiming philosophy as a universal human practice, the diversity of which cannot be sacrificed to meet the agenda of a few at the expense of the many, can be realized. As van Hensbroek (2013: 32) makes clear, "even when many 'others' become convinced that a certain mode of doing Philosophy is interesting and useful, that does not make this way of practicing Philosophy a universal standard. Philosophy is always there in the plural." Taking a decidedly flexible and open understanding of philosophy constitutes one of the major points of departure for world philosophies as an approach. It is our contention that within the world philosophies approach is located African philosophy as emancipation and practice. And within that, we should also find other voices from the world's many cultures. There is, as Kimmerle argues (1995: 143), a place for every culture and its ideas in this multiverse of humanity and indeed, a place on the table for every philosophy in this "multiversum of cultures."

Conclusion

In this chapter we have considered the emerging reality of the world philosophies approach and the promise it holds for philosophy going forward. We have illustrated this with an example of a growing subfield in African philosophy. Our articulation of African philosophy as pre-eminently an emancipative practice is a feature that is not restricted to this chapter: it bestrides the entire book. We have tried to look beyond the present and to envision a future defined by world philosophies, including openness to different approaches and understandings of the philosophical enterprise. In electing to speak of a future characterized by "different streams and multiple voices," we have also in that sense sought to recapture the need for every tradition of philosophy to acknowledge its own internal diversity, as well as its own incompleteness, and to underscore the importance of dialogue. For us, therefore, philosophy is a discipline that is continuously in the process of finding itself as the world evolves. It is a practice with its own contested history and an activity that is without end as long as there are reflective minds in the world. What it will become—including the various shapes and forms it will assume—is therefore something that no one can foretell with certainty. The emancipative struggle for philosophy in Africa is a process that is still ongoing and it will remain so as long as the injustices that pervade the epistemic landscape, including the world we live in, continues to undermine the dignity and well-being of others. The emancipative spirit that drives the practice of philosophy in Africa has to be strengthened in order for it to be able to respond adequately to new, emerging challenges, including the threats arising from the rehashing of old colonial prejudices. Confronting these challenges is something we owe to ourselves, those who have gone before us, and future generations. African philosophy is tied to these struggles and it is in part defined by that reality. Philosophy in Africa must be unwavering in its pursuit of genuine openness, including the need to reconfigure the philosophical enterprise itself. Ultimately, in this openness to others and in the world philosophies approach lies the answer to the question of what it means to be true to both philosophy and humanity.

Further Reading

This book is both an ongoing dialogue with history and an attempt to advance the discourse on world philosophies. It draws on the inherent emancipative mission that drives African philosophy within the context of the unfinished humanistic project of decolonization. It recognizes that for the African, and indeed for other similarly placed people in the world, true decolonization begins at the level of knowing oneself: it is about self-(re)discovery. We have shown that real philosophy moves forward not just by celebrating its successes, but by paying attention to some of its most serious failures and omissions. Our turn to world philosophies in the sense of reviving once more philosophy's multiple voices in dialogue is an attempt to demonstrate this crucial point. We have given from within African philosophy an example of Ubuntu philosophy as a tradition of thought which has now distinguished itself as a subfield within the discourse of African philosophy. It has its own distinctive approach and priority questions inspired by what it means to philosophize in an unjust world. Our contention is that with its grounding in the understanding of the universal oneness of humanity, this philosophy should be, within the spirit of world philosophies, made available to the world because within it is an understanding of philosophy capable of changing not only our relations as humans but also our relationship with the environment. This is an example of conceptual resources invaluable to humanity that are located in African philosophy; other indigenous philosophies of this world have equally valid intellectual resources that we should pay attention to as a people. It is important to emphasize that the world is changing and there are indications that once again it may be possible to celebrate philosophy as a widely shared practice and to return to philosophy its richness and diversity. The further reading list we provide below is in no way exhaustive but will give you an idea of what we have been trying to advance in this book. It should be clear to all that African philosophy is a growing discourse: it is continuing to unfold in many promising ways and the fecundity of its expression is adding to the stock of knowledge and concepts available to humanity.

Alongside the sources mentioned below we would encourage you to give considered attention to the following book for crucial insights on world philosophies:

Kirloskar-Steinbach, M., and L. Kalmanson (2021), *A Practical Guide to World Philosophies: Selves, Worlds, and Ways of Knowing,* London: Bloomsbury Publishing.

Chapter 1

Chapter One introduced some of the key issues in the history of African philosophy and familiarity with that history is crucial in making sense of the disputes that have characterized African philosophy regarding its methods and demarcation. There are a number of works that can be consulted to enhance one's knowledge of this history. In order to establish itself as a discipline, African philosophy had to contend with the politics of being an enterprise whose existence had been denied by demonstrating not only the fallacies of such a position, but also by establishing its own credentials as a philosophy. It was important to delineate the field and to protect it against disreputable works, charlatans and impostors. The famous critique of ethnophilosophy owes its origins to this effort. Today, almost every new entrant into the field of African philosophy as an academic study is introduced to "the critique of ethnophilosophy" as part of their initiation into the debate concerning its history and development.

Perhaps what is crucial for further engagement is to examine the different factors which have influenced the nature of African philosophy in terms of its outlook and preoccupation. The works identified here should help you not only to familiarize yourself with some of the debates that have ensued over the years, but also become more familiar with the issues we raised in the chapter.

Coetzee, P. H., and A. P. J. Roux, eds (2002), *Philosophy from Africa: A Text With Readings,* Cape Town: Oxford University Press of South Africa.

Hallen, B. (2002), *A Short History of African Philosophy,* Indiana: Indiana University Press.

Hallen, B. (2010), "Ethnophilosophy Redefined?" *Thought and Practice: A Journal of the Philosophical Association of Kenya,* 2 (1): 73–85.

Hountondji, P. J. (1996), *African Philosophy: Myth and Reality,* trans. H. Evans and J. Ree, Indianapolis: Indiana University Press.

Hountondji, P. (1989), "Occidentalism, Elitism: Answer to Two Critiques," trans. J. K. Chanda, *Quest: An African Journal of Philosophy,* 3 (2): 3–29.

Hountondji P. J. (2002), *The Struggle for Meaning: Reflections on Philosophy, Culture and Democracy in Africa*, trans. J. Conteh-Morgan, Athens, OH: Ohio University Center for International Studies.

Janz, B. (2009), *Philosophy in an African Place*, New York: Lexington Books.

Oruka, H. O., ed. (1991), *Sage Philosophy: Indigenous Thinkers and Modern Debate on African Philosophy*, Nairobi: ACTS Press.

Masolo, D. A. (1994), *African Philosophy in Search of Identity*, Indianapolis: Indiana University Press.

Masolo, D. A. (1997), "African Philosophy: A Historical Overview," in E. Deutsch and R. Bontekoe (eds.), *A Companion to World Philosophies*, 63–77, New York: Blackwell Publishers.

Masolo D. A. (2000), 'From Myth to Reality: African Philosophy at Century-end," *Research in African Literatures*, 31(1): 149–72.

Mungwini, P. (2019), "The Critique of Ethnophilosophy in the Mapping and Trajectory of African Philosophy," *Filosofia Theoretica: Journal of African Philosophy, Culture and Religions*, 8 (3): 1–20.

Outlaw, L. T., Jr (1992), "African, African American, Africana Philosophy," *The Philosophical Forum*, 24 (1–3): 63–93.

Ramose, M.B. (1999), *African Philosophy through Ubuntu*, Harare: Mond Books.

Serequeberhan T. (1991), *African Philosophy: The Essential Readings*, New York: Paragon House.

Wright, R. A., ed. (1984), *Philosophy: An Introduction*, Lanham, MD: University Press of America.

Yai, O. (1977), "Theory and Practice in African Philosophy: The Poverty of Speculative Philosophy," *Second Order: An African Journal of Philosophy*, 6 (2): 3–20.

Chapter 2

The history of philosophy as an exclusive and exclusionary discourse and its projection as a European gift to the world needs no further elaboration except to emphasize that the consequences of that skewed narrative are still with us today. However, the search for knowledge—and even truth—has never been the preserve of any one particular category or generation of human beings; its existence is evident throughout history and across cultures. In the chapter we have tried to highlight the consequences of a certain mode of understanding the business of philosophy which obscures the significance of Africa's indigenous oral resources to African philosophy. The latter must also (among other things) help its people to meet the imperative for the African to "know thyself." Focus on often-neglected intellectual resources must help to yield a philosophy distinctive not in terms of any difference in standards but rather in the questions it prioritizes and of course within the context of Africa's own historical circumstances.

The main issue in following up on what we have covered would be to try and identify both the internal and external factors that could account for the apparent challenges faced by African philosophers in being able to explore the philosophical resources inherent in their cultures. The reading list below should help to broaden your understanding of this issue and to see why we think that the traditional resources yet to be fully explored in African cultures should attract the interest of all philosophers.

Afolayan, A., and T. Falola, eds (2017) *The Palgrave handbook of African Philosophy*, New York: Palgrave Macmillan.

Gyekye, K. (1987), *An Essay on African Philosophical Thought. The Akan Conceptual Scheme,* Cambridge: Cambridge University Press.

Janz, B. (2009), *Philosophy in an African Place,* New York: Lexington Books.

Masolo, D. A. (2003), "Philosophy and Indigenous Knowledge: An African Perspective," *Africa Today.* 50 (2): 21–38.

Okere, T. (1983), *African Philosophy: A Historico-Hermeneutical Investigation of the Conditions of its Possibility,* Lanham, MD: University Press of America.

Ramose, M. B. (1999), *African Philosophy through Ubuntu.* Harare: Mond Books.

Serequeberhan, T. (1997), "The Critique of Eurocentrism and the Practice of African Philosophy," in E.C. Eze (ed.), *Postcolonial African Philosophy: A Critical Reader,* 141–61, London: Blackwell Publishers.

Serequeberhan, T. (2009), "African Philosophy As the Practice of Resistance," *Journal of Philosophy: A Cross-Disciplinary Inquiry*, 4 (9): 44–52.

Wiredu, K. (1980), *Philosophy and an African Culture,* Cambridge: Cambridge University Press.

Wiredu, K., and K. Gyekye, eds. (1992), *Person and Community: Ghanaian Philosophical Studies, 1,* Washington DC: Council for Research in Values and Philosophy.

Wiredu, K. (1996), *Cultural Universals and Particulars,* Bloomington: Indiana University Press.

Wiredu, K., ed. (2004), *A Companion to African Philosophy,* Oxford: Blackwell Publishing.

Chapter 3

As you may have seen already in the chapter, we chose to frame the discussion on intercultural philosophy around the question of what it means to be true to both philosophy and to humanity and what that entails for the practice of philosophy everywhere, including Africa. Our position is that there is a growing need for philosophical engagements *across* cultural boundaries. More significantly, it is becoming increasingly clear that the old anti-philosophical attitude which runs contrary to the very nature of philosophy as a universal human achievement is slowly diminishing in influence. In calling for the advancement of intercultural philosophizing, our point of departure is that there is no single tradition of philosophy that can consider itself as the only true philosophy for all humanity. Consistent with our argument for world philosophies, philosophy is there in multiple voices and it is this which renders dialogue across cultures indispensable to the practice of philosophy in today's world. To be true to both philosophy and to humanity, philosophical practice must transform itself into an arena defined not on the basis of any assumed hegemony, but on the basis of multiple voices in dialogue.

Again we propose that for further engagement on this topic it would perhaps be important to consider not only the factors that may militate against dialogue and which therefore ought to be overcome but also to propose the kind of topics around which dialogue across cultures can be held. In other words, we are looking here for examples of fertile areas of inter-philosophical dialogue and the philosophical outcomes they can yield. The books and articles below contain reflections that may assist you with this undertaking and with the main issues advocated by an intercultural approach to philosophy.

Balslev, A. N. (1996), *Cross-cultural Conversation*, Atlanta, GA: Scholars Press.

Bell, R. (2002), *Understanding African Philosophy: A Cross-Cultural Approach to Classical and Contemporary Issues*, London: Routledge.

Bernasconi, R. (1997), "Philosophy's paradoxical parochialism," in K. Ansell-Pearson, B. Perry, and J. Squires (eds.), *Cultural Readings of Imperialism:*

Edward Said and the Gravity of History, 212–26, London: Lawrence and Wishart.

Bernasconi, R. (1997), "African Philosophy's Challenge to Continental Philosophy," in E. C. Eze (ed.), *Postcolonial African Philosophy: A Critical Reader,* 183–96, Cambridge: Blackwell Publishers.

Bernasconi, R. (2003), "Ethnicity, Culture and Philosophy," in N. Bunnin and E. P. T. Tsui-James (eds.), *The Blackwell Companion to Philosophy,* 567–81, New York: Blackwell Publishers.

Dussel, E. (2009), "The New Age in the History of Philosophy," *Philosophy and Social Criticism,* 35 (5): 499–516.

Dussel, E. (2013), "Agenda for a South–South philosophical dialogue," *Human Architecture: Journal of the Sociology of Self-Knowledge,* 11 (1): 3–18.

Janz, B. (1997), "Alterity, Dialogue and African Philosophy," in E. C. Eze (ed.), *Postcolonial African Philosophy: A Critical Reader*, 221–38, Oxford: Blackwell Publishers.

Janz, B. (2015), "Philosophy-in-Place and the Provenance of Dialogue," *South African Journal of Philosophy*, 34 (4): 480–90.

Kirloskar-Steinbach, M., G. Raman, and J. Maffie, (2014), "Introducing Confluence: A Thematic Essay," *Confluence: Journal of World Philosophies*, 1: 7–63.

Mall, R. A. (2014), "Intercultural Philosophy: A Conceptual Clarification," *Confluence: Journal of World Philosophies*, 1: 67–84.

Mungwini, P. (2015), "Dialogue As the Negation of Hegemony: An African Perspective," *South African Journal of Philosophy,* 34 (4): 395–407.

Mungwini P. (2019), "The Quest for Epistemic Liberation: What Can Be Done to Be True to Both Philosophy and to Humanity?" *Journal of World Philosophies*, 4: 70–7.

Vest, J. L. (2005), "The Promise of Caribbean Philosophy: How It Can Contribute to a 'New Dialogic' in Philosophy," *Caribbean Studies,* 33 (2): 3–34.

Wimmer, F. M. (2002), *Essays on Intercultural Philosophy,* Chennai: Satya Nilayam Publications.

Wimmer F. M. (2015), "How Are Histories of Non-Western Philosophies Relevant to Intercultural Philosophizing?" *Confluence: Online Journal of World Philosophies* 3: 124–32.

Wiredu, K. (1996), *Cultural Universals and Particulars.* Bloomington: Indiana University Press.

Wiredu, K. (1998), "Can Philosophy Be Intercultural? An African Viewpoint," *Diogenes,* 46 (4): 147–67.

Chapter 4

The debate over the decolonization of knowledge has arisen against the reality of the continued marginalization of other traditions of knowledge, and should be tied to the struggle for global justice. The imperative to reconfigure the epistemic landscape, and to restore meaning and identity to those who have suffered exclusion and marginalization, is central to the African philosophical project. It is a call to assume responsibility for this corrective intervention in order to ensure that the particularity of the African experiences and indeed those of other indigenous peoples of this world shall never again be unduly smothered or suffocated under the weight of a hegemonic universalism. The idea is to recenter Africa, placing it in charge of its own destiny and helping it on the path to intellectual independence. For illustrative purposes, we have drawn attention to the "Rhodes Must Fall" movement as an example of an emancipative struggle belonging to the same category as other counter-hegemonic struggles like epistemologies of the global South. This epistemic struggle involves taking a closer look at the philosophical canon and other mechanisms to overcome constraints imposed on the practice through interventions such as conceptual decolonization and strategic particularism. The aim is to accord voice to the voiceless and, ultimately, help create a world without epistemic hegemony.

Here we have looked at a specific concern which reaches beyond philosophy and affects other disciplines in equal measure. Further critical issues for consideration might be proposals for how philosophy itself can be decolonized. Getting to the bottom of these conundrums is integral to understanding African philosophy, its struggles, and its future direction. The publications below examine some of these issues.

Allman, J. (2013), "Kwame Nkrumah, African Studies, and the Politics of Knowledge Production in the Black Star of Africa," *The International Journal of African Historical Studies*, 46 (2): 181–203.

Chemhuru, M. (2016), "Pursuing the Agenda of Africanising Philosophy in Africa: Some Possibilities," *South African Journal of Philosophy*, 35 (4): 418–28.

Dladla, N. (2017), "Racism and the Marginality of African philosophy in South Africa," *Phronimon,* 18: 204–31.

Gordon, L. R. (2019), "Decolonizing Philosophy," *The Southern Journal of Philosophy*, 57: 16–36.

Graness, A. (2015), "Questions of Canon Formation in Philosophy: The History of Philosophy in Africa," *Phronimon*, 16 (2): 78–96.

Hountondji, P. J. (2002), "Producing Knowledge in Africa Today," in P. Coetzee and A. Roux (eds.), *Philosophy from Africa: A Text with Readings,* 501–07, Cape Town: Oxford University Press of South Africa.

Hountondji, P. J. (2009), "Knowledge of Africa, Knowledge by Africans: Two Perspectives on African Studies," *RCCS Annual Review*, 1, 1–11.

Kebede, M. (2004), *Africa's Quest for a Philosophy of Decolonization,* Amsterdam: Rodopi.

Masaka, D. (2017), "Challenging Epistemicide through Tansformation and Africanisation of the Philosophy Curriculum," *South African Journal of Philosophy*, 36 (4): 441–55.

Monahan, M. (2019), "Reflections on Decolonizing Philosophy: Can there be Universality Without Universalism?" *Journal of World Philosophies* 4: 82–6.

Monahan, M. (2019), "Editor's introduction," *The Southern Journal of Philosophy*, 57: 5–15.

More, P. (2004), "Philosophy in South Africa under and after Apartheid," in K. Wiredu (ed.), *A Companion to African Philosophy*, 149–160, Oxford: Blackwell Publishing.

Mungwini, P. (2016), "The Question of Recentring Africa: Thoughts and Issues from the Global South," *South African Journal of Philosophy*, 35 (4): 523–36.

Mungwini, P. (2017), "African Know Thyself: Epistemic Injustice and the Quest for Liberative Knowledge," *International Journal of African Renaissance Studies- Multi-, Inter- and Transdiscipinarity*, 12 (2): 5–18.

Mungwini, P. (2021), "Decolonisation Debates in Higher Education," in A. Ndofirepi and E. T. Gwaravanda (eds.), *African Higher Education in the 21st Century: Some Philosophical Dimensions,* 106–21, Leiden: Brill.

Ndofirepi, P. A. and E. T. Gwaravanda (2019), "Epistemic (In)justice in African Universities: A Perspective of the Politics of Knowledge," *Educational Review*, 71 (5): 581–94.

Nkrumah, K. (1964), *Consciencism: Philosophy and Ideology for Decolonization and Development with Particular Reference to the African Revolution,* New York: Modern Reader Paperbacks.

Okere, T. (2005), "Is There One Science, Western Science?" *Africa Development*, 30 (3): 20–34.

Ramose, M. B. (2015), "On the Contested Meaning of Philosophy," *South African Journal of Philosophy* 34 (4): 551–8.

Serequeberhan, T. (1994), *The Hermeneutics of African Philosophy: Horizon and Discourse,* New York: Routledge.

Wa Thiong'o, N. (1987), *Decolonising the Mind: The Politics of Language in African Literatures,* Harare: Zimbabwe Publishing House.

Wiredu, K. (2002), "On Decolonizing African Religions," in P. H. Coetzee and A. P. J. Roux, (eds.), *Philosophy from Africa: A Text with Readings,* 20–34, Cape Town: Oxford University Press of South Africa.

Chapter 5

While philosophy is yet to recover fully from its troubled past, the direction it has taken in recent years is indeed promising. We have drawn attention to the promise that philosophy holds—that is, its yet-to-be-achieved potential as a universal enterprise. Our point is that there is emerging a new era of world philosophies stripped of the hegemony of any one particular tradition of thought, and within that schema is located all the different modes of understanding the world and our place within it. We have made use of the analogy of different streams and rivers that traverse the different territories in order to capture the plurality of philosophical traditions that constitute our reflective heritage as humanity. Special focus is placed on Ubuntu emancipative philosophy as a tradition of thought and a subfield within the discourse of African philosophy. It is a tradition of philosophy which resonates with the thinking of those who see philosophy as consubstantial with liberation. Over the years, however, the main problem has been that different philosophies have not been allowed to speak for themselves; even their "membership" to philosophy family was dependent on the decision of the dominant tradition. Ultimately, our concern revolves around how humanity can harness the emancipative spirit informed by the philosophy of Ubuntu towards a genuine worldwide project that serves the interests of the marginalized, the dispossessed, and the poor. Progress towards a richer and more complex understanding of philosophy, which recognizes the fecundity of philosophical expression, is in keeping not only with our diversity as thinkers, but also with the diversity of our cultures as the material resources out of which philosophy is nourished. We must, in agreement with the objectives of the world philosophies approach, reconfigure our sense of what it means to do philosophy in a plural and diverse world.

Again, it is vital to assess the promise of world philosophies and to determine whether it is not time to celebrate the waning grip of orthodoxy. Each of the readings listed below attempt—in their different ways—to speak to this reality, remaining conscious of the fact that it is still unfolding around us.

Bontekoe, R. (2017), "Some Opening Remarks on the Exclusionary Tendency in Western Philosophy," *Philosophy East and West*, 67 (4): 957–65.

Davis, B. W. (2017a), "Dislodging Eurocentrism and Racism from Philosophy," *Comparative and Continental Philosophy*, 9 (2): 115–18.

Edelglass, W., and J. L. Garfield (2011), "Introduction," in W. Edelglass and J. L. Garfield (eds.), *The Oxford Handbook of World Philosophy*, 3–6, www.oxfordhandbooks.com. Accessed August 5, 2020.

Ganeri, J. (2016), "Manifesto for a Re-emergent Philosophy," *Confluence: An Online Journal of World Philosophies*, 4: 134–142.

Garfield J. L., and W. Bryan Van Norden (2016), 'If Philosophy Won't Diversify, Let's Call It What It Really Is," https://www.nytimes.com/2016/05/11/opinion/if-philosophy-wont-diversify-lets-call-it-what-it-really-is.html. Accessed October 1, 2020.

Kirloskar-Steinbach, M. (2019), "Diversifying Philosophy: The Art of Non-domination," *Educational Philosophy and Theory*, 51 (14): 1490–1503.

Kirloskar-Steinbach, M., and L. Kalmanson (2021), *A Practical Guide to World Philosophies: Selves, Worlds, and Ways of Knowing*, London: Bloomsbury Publishing.

Praeg, L., and S. Magadla, eds (2014), *Ubuntu: Curating the Archive*, Pietermaritzburg: UKZN Press.

Smart, N. (1999), *World Philosophies*, London: Routledge.

Solomon, R. C. (2001), "What is Philosophy? The Status of World Philosophy in the Profession," *Philosophy East and West*, 51 (1): 100–04.

Strickland, L. (2018), "Western Philosophy Departments Must Open Their Minds," Metro https://www.mmu.ac.uk/news-and-events/news/story/?id=7283. Accessed October 1, 2020.

Strickland, L. (2019), "How Western Philosophy Became Racist," IAI News, https://iai.tv/articles/the-racism-of-the-western-philosophy-canon-auid-1200. Accessed October 1, 2020.

Finally, for more information on all the topics we have covered in this book, visit the website "History of Philosophy Without Any Gaps" (https://historyofphilosophy.net) and navigate to the section on "Africana philosophy" for podcasts and reading resources.

Notes

Introduction: The Emancipative Mission

1 The phrase is from Rettova (2016: 127).

2 See Outlaw (1992: 71)

3 https://en.wikipedia.org/wiki/Anton_Wilhelm_Amo. Kant (1724–1804) and Hegel (1770–1831) are two individuals renowned for their damaging views on Africa. Given the times in which they lived, it is surprising that they had not known or heard of Amo (1703–59), that African man, philosopher, and at one time teacher at the University of Jena, but of course we can only surmise that his intellectual record could not have stood for anything, particularly in view of what they had set themselves to do. His work was deliberately erased—or conveniently overlooked—in order to give effect to one of the greatest lies in the history of humanity. It is of great significance to learn that the proposal to name one of the famous streets in Germany after him is being considered. Whether it actually comes to pass matters less. The important thing is this historical initiative and all that it stands for as a testament to his contribution to our shared patrimony of knowledge. For this story, see, https://www.theguardian.com/world/2020/aug/21/berlin-rename-mohrenstrasse-moor-street-black-philosopher-anton-wilhelm-amo Accessed September 1, 2020.

4 For clarity, there is no harm in revisiting the following address by the Rector of the University of Wittenberg on the occasion of Amo's successful defense of his second Dissertation, courtesy of Abraham (1996) and cited in Hallen (2002: 10–11). It bears testimony to Amo's achievements and reads: "He won the affection of the Order of Philosophy to such an extent that by the unanimous vote of the Fathers [examiners], he was decorated with the laurels of philosophy. The honour won by the deserts of his ability, of his outstanding uprightness, industry, erudition, which he has shown by public and private exercises, he increased with praise. By his behaviour with the best and most learned, he acquired great influence; among his equals, he easily shone out. . . . Having examined the opinions of the ancients as well as the moderns, he garnered all that was best, and what he

picked out he interpreted with precision and with lucidity. This work
proved that his intellectual ability was as great as his powers of teaching."

1 The Terrain of African Philosophy

1   See for example Matolino's 2019 essay "Ethnophilosophy as a Dead
    Discourse," a title that captures the essence of his argument in the piece.
    But it may be the case that the dead *do* speak. Controversies surrounding
    the critique may have invested ethnophilosophy with a certain form of
    recalcitrance, if not a tinge of immortality, within the discourse of African
    philosophy. In our view, the fact that people may agree that the book is
    catastrophically misconceived does not render it irrelevant to African
    philosophy. In other words, its continued relevance may lie in that very fact
    of its being an example of how not to proceed on one hand and on the
    other as a work without which the history of African philosophy would be
    difficult to understand.
2   We can indeed confirm at this point that an issue featuring that debate was
    published in 2019 with the title "Are We Finished with the
    Ethnophilosophy Debate? A Multi-perspective Conversation." The debate
    features eight philosophers who offer their different voices and
    perspectives on this topic. Of course, our own interest is of a different
    nature. It is to assess the aftermath of this crucial critique and specifically
    the potentially negative impact that the critique may have had on African
    philosophy.
3   Still on this point, it may be appropriate to add the view carried in a
    footnote by Appiah (1992: 203, fn. 47) which makes it clear that even the
    position that ethnophilosophy had nothing to do with philosophy was
    overstated.
4   This we say in order to point to what is seemingly an inconsistency. For in
    the very same book, but now dealing with a different author Hountondji
    (1996: 180) writes, "it is . . . disastrous. . . to flatten a work by stripping it of
    its tensions, of its evolution, by abstracting it from its historical context and
    the concrete problems it strove to solve." The question is: Could he maybe
    have applied the same principle to Tempels's work? Perhaps, and for the
    many of us who can only read English, a meticulous rereading of Tempels

along the lines suggested in the little-known article by Willem Storm (1993) *Bantoe-Filosofe vs Bantu Philosophy* is after all necessary, where particular care is taken to compare the now-popular English translation against the original version involving not only the English version's preference for specific degrading terminologies and omissions. Attention should also be paid to (foot)notes, which seem distinct from the original version in the manner in which they seem to add to the text's negativity.

5   It refers to the ideal penitentiary structure (designed by Bentham), in which only the supervisor can see all the inmates, none of whom are able to see him. Here, even when the supervisor is absent from the control room, social deviance could be controlled around the clock with minimum force and manpower under the pretext of an omnipresent supervisor. The panopticon creates within the minds of the inmates the feeling that they are being constantly watched, even when the supervisor is absent. From this consciousness, the inmates develop self-regulated conformity and control over their behavior all the time. This, we submit, is among some of the negative effects the critique had on the minds of fellow African philosophers, and in particular on the young who may have contemplated defining a path of their own into the enterprise.

6   See Lucius Outlaw (1996: 13), on why there is need to consider the etymological sense of the term.

7   Although we make explicit reference to Hountondji in this chapter, he was by no means alone on this journey. Several of his contemporaries were just some of those who followed him, reinforcing the position. We have only considered what we called the potentially crippling side of the critique, but much can also be said regarding the indisputably positive contribution that the critique has brought to the field of African philosophy.

8   The phrase is taken from Appiah (1992: 88).

2 African Self-Apprehension

1   Given the manner in which this subject features occasionally in discussions on African philosophy, it is important that we refer again to Wiredu and somehow cite his position at length. In our view, he has managed to demonstrate through his own practice of philosophy that

communal philosophy, or particularistic studies of the philosophies of different ethnic groups, is not incompatible nor antithetical to philosophy. According to Wiredu (1998: 25): "The very idea of a communal philosophy that is entailed in the notion of particularistic studies of traditional African philosophies might be put in question. It might be suggested that to talk of the Bantu conception of this or the Zulu conception of that is to postulate a unanimity or consensus in philosophical belief among the traditional peoples for which there is not, and probably can never be, sufficient evidence. It is necessary, in response to this, to explain at once that talk of the communal philosophy of an ethnic group does not necessarily imply that the conceptions involved are entertained by all members of the group. What it means is that anybody thoughtfully knowledgeable about the culture will know that such conceptions are customary in the culture though s/he may not subscribe to it. The evidence for a communal philosophy is very much like that for the customs of a culture. In fact, in quite some cases customs are encapsulations of some aspects of a communal philosophy."

3 Philosophy and Intercultural Dialogue

1 The question is a slight modification of the one raised by Okere (2005: 33).
2 In their article featured in *The New York Times* entitled "If Philosophy Won't Diversify, Let's Call It What It Really Is," Jay L Garfield and Bryan W Van Norden, having painted the picture of how the vast majority of philosophy departments in the United States have neglected the teaching of philosophy courses from non-European traditions, state: "Given the importance of non-European traditions in both the history of world philosophy and in the contemporary world, and given the increasing numbers of students in our Colleges and universities from non-European backgrounds, this is astonishing. No other humanities discipline demonstrates this systematic neglect of most of the civilizations in its domain. The present situation is hard to justify morally, politically, epistemically or as good educational and research training practice." https://www.nytimes.com/2016/05/11/opinion/if-philosophy-wont-diversify-lets-call-it-what-it-really-is.html. Accessed October 1, 2020.

3 See Lloyd Strickland, 2018, https://www.mmu.ac.uk/news-and-events/news/story/?id=7283. Accessed October 1, 2020.
4 Lloyd Strickland, How Western Philosophy Became Racist, published January 10, 2019. https://iai.tv/articles/the-racism-of-the-western-philosophy-canon-auid-1200. Accessed October 1, 2020.
5 Ibid.
6 The phrase is taken from Serequeberhan (2011: 473).

4 Recentering Africa: The Unfinished Promise of Decolonization

1 This is a term used by Wiredu (1996: 145) to refer to "the first wave of rulers in post-independence Africa ... who had led successful anti-colonial struggles which were as much cultural as they were political. [Among these leaders are the likes of] Nkrumah of Ghana, Senghor of Senegal, Sékou Touré of Guinea, Nyerere of Tanzania, and Kaunda of Zambia [who put forward] blueprints of politics and development based on general conceptions of community, polity, and the general good ... some like Nkrumah and Senghor had technical training in philosophy. But others, such as Kaunda, had only their enlightened intuitions to rely on. ... Nevertheless, in every case it was historical circumstance that made them philosopher-kings."
2 The First and Second Congress of Negro Writers and Artists, both held in the 1950s, are regarded as landmark conferences which brought together leading black intellectuals for the purposes of addressing issues of colonialism and racism, and to consolidate the fight for decolonization.
3 See the following two websites: http://rhodesmustfall.co.za/ as well as https://rmfoxford.wordpress.com/about/ Accessed March 23, 2016.
4 "Rhodes Must Fall in Oxford." https://rmfoxford.wordpress.com/about/. Accessed March 23, 2016.
5 "Otto Neurath, Stanford Encyclopaedia of Philosophy." https://plato.stanford.edu/entries/neurath/. Accessed February 15, 2021.
6 The term is borrowed from Wiredu (1998: 28).
7 For this phrase and a detailed articulation of the problem, see Outlaw (2007: 197).

5 Africa and World Philosophies: The Emerging Realities

1 The idea of the analogy of different rivers and streams is borrowed from Ngugi wa Thiong'o (2012: 55–6), who uses it with reference to the question of world literature.

2 With this we capture two related meanings, that is, Ubuntu as an indigenous African moral theory on one hand and Ubuntu as a politico-ideological concept on the other. From these two has emerged an emancipative tradition of philosophy in African philosophy with its own distinct way of approaching the practice of philosophy, just as we speak of other traditions of thought such as the Latin American Philosophy of Liberation. In this subfield of philosophy, which appropriately defines the Ubuntu tradition of philosophy, the two understandings of Ubuntu intertwine to constitute the foundation upon which this tradition and practice of philosophy is built.

3 The term comes from Janz's essay, "Philosophy-in-Place and the provenance of dialogue" (2015: 480).

4 Kwame Nkrumah (1967), "African Socialism Revisited." https://www.marxists.org/subject/africa/nkrumah/1967/african-socialism-revisited.htm Accessed March 9, 2021.

5 Kimmerle Heinz, "A New Approach to African Philosophy: Mogobe B Ramose: African Philosophy Through Ubuntu', Book Review." http://www.galerie-inter.de/kimmerle/Text4.htm Accessed March 10, 2021.

6 For those particularly interested in exploring this dimension of African philosophy, we would encourage you to read Ramose's numerous writings over the years. Another dimension of this philosophy also receives closer discussion in an article by Ndumiso Dladla (2017a) on Ubuntu as a philo-praxis of liberation, where he submits that as a philosophy of liberation, Ubuntu can form a solid philosophical-anthropological foundation for an African Critical Philosophy of Race.

7 In a recent essay Oguejiofor (2019: 119), identifies Ramose as "one of the most prominent contemporary [...] African philosophers whose work shows a deep understanding of the contextual challenge which is essential to philosophising." For example, he draws attention to the way Ramose has brought his interpretation of Ubuntu to bear on the question of justice for

the indigenous people of Africa who have suffered dispossession and systemic exclusion since the colonial conquest.

8   An organization which describes itself as a global environmental movement with the stated aim of using nonviolent civil disobedience to compel government action to avoid tipping points in the climate system, biodiversity loss, and the risk of social and ecological collapse. See https://en.wikipedia.org/wiki/Extinction_Rebellion Accessed March 10, 2021.

9   The meaning of the three proverbs in that order can be rendered as follows: "to be human is to affirm one's humanity by recognizing the humanity of others and, on that basis, establish humane relations with them"; "if and when one is faced with a decisive choice between wealth and the preservation of the life of another human being, then one should opt for the preservation of life"; "the king owes his status, including all the powers associated with it, to the will of the people under him".

10 This indigenous aphorism also features prominently in, and is foundational to, Ramose's engagement with questions of historical justice and in particular colonial dispossession of land through conquest in unjust wars. Philosophically, the indigenous peoples hold that *molato ga o bole,* that is, extinctive prescription, is untenable in the African understanding of law (Ramose 2002; 2018). On the issue of land, equilibrium must be restored through the restoration of title to territory and sovereignty over it to its rightful owners, the indigenous peoples of Africa. This same indigenous principle would apply with equal significance to the question of reparations, since it is only through such a process that the crimes against Africa could be addressed.

11 See Ramose (2001), "An African perspective on justice and race", Polylog: https://them.polylog.org/3/frm-en.htm Accessed May 26, 2021. His position is that: "The ubuntu understanding of justice as the restoration of equilibrium means that law as a continually lived experience cannot reach a point of finality. Accordingly, prescription is unknown in African law. The African believes that time cannot change the truth. Just as the truth must be taken into consideration each time it becomes known, so must no obstacle be placed in the way of the search for it and its discovery." Ramose submits that, concerning the question of land in South Africa today, there is no justice until and unless equilibrium is restored through the restoration of title to territory and the reversion of sovereignty over it.

References

Afolayan, A. (2018), "Abiola Irele and the Context of African Philosophy Discourse," *Research in African Literatures*, 49 (2): 1–19.

Alcoff, L. M. (2007), "Mignolo's Epistemology of Coloniality," *CR: The Centennial Review*, 7 (3): 79–101.

Allman, J. (2013), "Kwame Nkrumah, African Studies and the Politics of Knowledge Production in the Black Star of Africa," *The International Journal of African Historical Studies*, 46 (2): 181–203.

Appiah, K. A. (1992), *In My Father's House*, Oxford: Oxford University Press.

Appiah, K. A. (2010), "Europe Upside Down: Fallacies of the New Afrocentrism," in R. C. Grinker, S. C. Lubkemann, and C. Steiner (eds.), *Perspectives on Africa: A Reader in Culture, History and Representation*, 48–54, Oxford: Wiley-Blackwell.

Arisaka, Y. (2001), "The Status of Asian and Asian-American Philosophers and Philosophies," *APA Newsletter*, 1 (1): 25–25.

Asante, M. K. (2003), "The Afrocentric Idea," in A. Mazama (ed.), *The Afrocentric Paradigm*, 36–53, Asmara: Africa World Press.

Banuri, T. (2011), "Development and the Politics of Knowledge: A Critical interpretation of the Social Role of Modernization Theories in the Development of the Third World," *Oxford Scholarship Online*. Available at: www.oxfordscholaship.com. (Accessed May 13, 2016.)

Bell, R. (1989), "Narrative in African Philosophy," *Philosophy*. 64 (249): 363–79.

Bernasconi, R. (1995), "Heidegger and the Invention of the Western Philosophical Tradition," *Journal of the British Society for Phenomenology*, 26 (3): 240–54.

Bernasconi, R. (1997), "Philosophy's paradoxical parochialism," in K. Ansell-Pearson, B. Perry, and J. Squires (eds.), *Cultural Readings of Imperialism. Edward Said and the Gravity of History*, 212–26, London: Lawrence and Wishart.

Bernasconi, R. (1997a), "African Philosophy's Challenge to Continental Philosophy," in E. C. Eze (ed.), *Postcolonial African Philosophy: A Critical Reader*, 183–96, Cambridge: Blackwell Publishers.

Bernasconi, R. (2000), "Almost Always More Than Philosophy Proper," *Research in Phenomenology*, 30: 1–11.

Bernasconi, R. (2003), "Ethnicity, Culture and Philosophy," in N. Bunnin and E. P. T. Tsui-James (eds.), *The Blackwell Companion to Philosophy*, 567–81, New York: Blackwell Publishers.

Biney, A. (2014), "The Historical Discourse on African Humanism: Interrogating the Paradoxes," in L. Praeg and S. Magadla (eds.), *Ubuntu: Curating the Archive*, 27–53, Pietermaritzburg: UKZN Press.

Bourdillon, M. (1987), *The Shona Peoples: An Ethnography of the Contemporary Shona with Special Reference to their Religion*, Gweru: Mambo Press.

Bontekoe, R. (2017), "Some Opening Remarks on the Exclusionary Tendency in Western Philosophy," *Philosophy East and West*, 67 (4): 957–65.

Brueggemann, W. (1977), *The Land: Place as Gift, Promise, and Challenge in Biblical Faith*, Philadelphia: Fortress Press.

Bruns, G. L. (1984), "Canon and Power in the Hebrew Scriptures," *Critical Inquiry*, 10 (3): 462–80.

Bujo, B. (1998), *The Ethical Dimension of Community: The African Model and the Dialogue Between North and South*, Nairobi: Paulines Publications Africa.

Chimakonam, J. O. (2015), "Transforming the African Philosophical Place Through Conversations: An Inquiry into the Global Expansion of Thought (GET)," *South African Journal of Philosophy*, 34 (4): 462–79.

Chimakonam J. O., and V. C. Nweke (2018), "Why the 'Politics' Against African Philosophy Should Be Discontinued," *Dialogue: Canadian Philosophical Review*, 57 (2): 277–301.

Chitando, E., and F. Mangena (2015), "Philosophy in the 'House of Stone': A Critical Review," *South African Journal of Philosophy*, 34 (2); 226–39.

Davis, B. W. (2017), "Gadfly of Continental Philosophy: On Robert Bernasconi's Critique of Philosophical Eurocentrism," *Comparative and Continental Philosophy*, 9 (2): 119–29.

Davis, B. W. (2017a), "Dislodging Eurocentrism and Racism from Philosophy," *Comparative and Continental Philosophy*, 9 (2): 115–18.

Dladla, N. (2017), "Racism and the Marginality of African philosophy in South Africa," *Phronimon*, 18: 204–31.

Dladla, N. (2017a), "Towards an African Critical Philosophy of Race: Ubuntu as a Philo-praxis of Liberation," *Filosofia Theoretica: Journal of African philosophy, Culture and Religions*, 6 (1): 39–68.

Dryden, J. (2018), "Guest Editor's introduction: 'Philosophy and its borders,'" *Dialogue: Canadian Philosophical Review*, 57 (2): 203–16.

Dubgen, F., and S. Skupien (2019), *Paulin Hountondji: Global Political Thinkers*, Palgrave: Macmillan.

Dussel, E. (2008), *Twenty Theses on Politics*, Durham, NC: Duke University Press.

Dussel, E. (2013), "Agenda for a South–South Philosophical Dialogue," *Human Architecture: Journal of the Sociology of Self-Knowledge*, 11 (1): 3–18.

Edelglass, W., and J. L. Garfield (2011), "Introduction," in W. Edelglass and J. L. Garfield (eds.), *The Oxford Handbook of World Philosophy*, 3–6, www.oxfordhandbooks.com. Accessed August 5, 2020.

Eze, C. E. (1997), "The Color of Reason: The Idea of 'Race' in Kant's Anthropology," in C .E. Eze (ed.), *Postcolonial African Philosophy: A Critical Reader*, 103–140, Cambridge: Blackwell Publishers.

Eze, C. (2015), "Decolonisation and Its Discontents: Thoughts on the Postcolonial African Moral Self," *South African Journal of Philosophy*, 34 (4): 408–18.

Eze, M. O., and T. Metz (2015), "Emergent Issues in African Philosophy: A Dialogue with Wiredu," *Philosophia Africana*, 17 (2): 75–87.

Flory, D. (2017), "Race, History, and Affect: Comments on Peter K.J. Park's 'Africa, Asia, and the History of Philosophy'," *Journal of World Philosophies*, 2: 48–59.

Foucault, M. (1998), "Polemics, Politics and Problematization," in P. Rabinow (ed.), *Essential Works of Foucault*, 381–90, New York: The New Press.

Ganeri, J. (2016), "Manifesto for a Re-emergent Philosophy," *Confluence: An Online Journal of World Philosophies*, 4, 134–42.

Garfield J. L., and W. Bryan Van Norden (2016), "If Philosophy Won't Diversify, Let's Call It What It Really Is," https://www.nytimes.com/2016/05/11/opinion/if-philosophy-wont-diversify-lets-call-it-what-it-really-is.html. (Accessed October 1, 2020.)

Gieryn, T. F. (1999), *Cultural Boundaries of Science: Credibility on the Line*, Chicago: University of Chicago Press.

Gordon, L. R. (2014), "Disciplinary Decadence and the Decolonisation of Knowledge," *Africa Development*, 39 (1): 81–92.

Gordon, L. R. (2019), "Decolonising Philosophy," *The Southern Journal of Philosophy*, 57: 16–36.

Gracia, J. J. E. (1992), *Philosophy and its History: Issues in Philosophical Historiography*, New York: State University of New York Press.

Graness, A. (2015), "Questions of Canon Formation in Philosophy: The History of Philosophy in Africa," *Phronimon*, 16 (2): 78–96.

Gyekye, K. (1987), *An Essay on African Philosophical Thought: The Akan Conceptual Scheme*, Cambridge: Cambridge University Press.

Hallen, B. (2002), *A Short History of African Philosophy*, Indianapolis: Indiana University Press.

Hallen, B. (2010), "Ethnophilosophy Redefined?" *Thought and Practice: A Journal of the Philosophical Association of Kenya*, 2 (1): 73–85.

Hallen, B. (2019), "Be-ing and Being Ramose," in H. Lauer, and H. Yitah (eds.), *The Tenacity of Truthfulness: Philosophical Essays in Honour of Mogobe Bernard Ramose*, 13–20, Dar –es- Salaam: Mkuki na Nyota.

Hallen, B. (2021), *Reading Wiredu*, Bloomington: Indiana University Press.

Harris, V. W. (1991), "Canonicity," *PMLA—Modern Language Association*, 106 (1): 110–21.

Hart, M. A. (2010), "Indigenous Worldviews, Knowledge, and Research: The Development of an Indigenous Research Paradigm," *Journal of Indigenous Voices in Social Work*, 1 (1): 1–16.

Healy, P. (2013), "Overcoming Incommensurability Through Intercultural Dialogue," *Cosmos and History: The Journal of Natural and Social Philosophy*, 9 (1): 265–81.

Hein, H. (1993), "Institutional Blessing: The Museum as Canon-maker," *The Monist*, 76 (4): 556–73.

Hountondji, P. J. (1989), "Occidentalism, Elitism: Answer to Two Critiques," trans. J. K. Chanda, *Quest: An African Journal of Philosophy*, 3 (2): 3–29.

Houtondji, P. J. (1996), *African Philosophy: Myth and Reality*, trans. H. Evans and J. Ree, Indianapolis: Indiana University Press.

Hountondji P. J. (2002), *The Struggle for Meaning: Reflections on Philosophy, Culture and Democracy in Africa*, trans. J. Conteh-Morgan, Athens, OH: Ohio University Center for International Studies.

Hountondji, P. J. (2002a), "Producing Knowledge in Africa Today," in P. Coetzee and A. Roux (eds), *Philosophy from Africa: A Text with Readings*, 501–07, Oxford: Oxford University Press.

Hountondji, P. J. 2009. "Knowledge of Africa, Knowledge by Africans: Two Perspectives on African studies," *RCCS Annual Review*, 1:1–11

Hountondji, P. J. (2018), "How African is Philosophy in Africa?" *Filosofia Theoretica: Journal of African Philosophy, Culture and Religions*, 7 (3): 9–18.

Hutton, S. (2019), "Women, Philosophy and the History of Philosophy," *British Journal for the History of Philosophy*, 27 (4): 684–701.

Irele, A. (1996), "Introduction," in P. J. Houtodji, *African Philosophy: Myth and Reality*, 7–30, Indianapolis: Indiana University Press.

Janz, B. (1997), "Alterity, Dialogue and African philosophy," in E. C. Eze (ed.), *Postcolonial African Philosophy: A Critical Reader*, 221–38, Oxford: Blackwell Publishers.

Janz, B. (2009), *Philosophy in an African Place*, New York: Lexington Books.

Janz, B. (2015), "Philosophy-in-Place and the Provenance of Dialogue," *South African Journal of Philosophy*, 34 (4): 480–90.

Janz, B. (2017), "The Geography of African Philosophy," in A. Afolayan and T. Falola, (eds), *The Palgrave Handbook of African Philosophy*, 55–166, New York: Palgrave Macmillan.

Jenlink P. M., and B. H. Banathy, (2005), "Dialogue: Conversation as Culture Building and Consciousness Evolving," in B. H. Benathy and P. M. Jenlink (eds.), *Dialogue as a Means of Collective Communication*, 3–14, New York: Kluwer Academic Publishers.

Jones, W. E., and T. Metz, (2015), "The Politics of Philosophy in Africa: A Conversation," *South African Journal of Philosophy*, 34 (4): 538–50.

Kalmanson, L. (2017), "Decolonizing the Department: Peter K. J. Park and the Profession of Philosophy," *Journal of World Philosophies*, 2: 60–5.

Kermode, F. (1979), "Institutional Control of Interpretation," *Salmagundi*, 43: 72–86.

Kimmerle, H. (1995) "The Multiversum of Cultures: The Mutual Relations Between the Cultures and the End of Modernity," *Hitotsubashi Journal of Social Studies*, 27: 143–150.

Kimmerle, H. (n.d), "A New Approach to African Philosophy: Mogobe B Ramose: African Philosophy Through Ubuntu," Book Review. http://www.galerie-inter.de/kimmerle/Text4.htm. (Accessed March 10, 2021.)

Kirloskar-Steinbach, M., G. Raman, and J. Maffie, (2014), "Introducing Confluence: A Thematic Essay," *Confluence: Journal of World Philosophies*, 1: 7–63.

Kirloskar-Steinbach, M. (2019), "Diversifying Philosophy: The Art of Non-domination," *Educational Philosophy and Theory*, 51 (14): 1490–1503.

Kirloskar-Steinbach, M., and L. Kalmanson (2021), *A Practical Guide to World Philosophies: Selves, Worlds, and Ways of Knowing*, London: Bloomsbury Publishing.

Ki-Zerbo, J. (1981), "General Introduction," in J. Ki-Zerbo (ed.), *UNESCO General History of Africa Volume 1*, 1–23, UNESCO: University of California Press.

Kovel, J. (2014), "Ecosocialism As a Human Phenomenon," *Capitalism Nature Socialism* 25 (1): 10–23.

Kresse, K. (2002), "Towards an Anthropology of Philosophies: Four Turns, with Reference to the African Context," in G. M. Presby et al (eds.), *Thought and Practice in African Philosophy*, 29–46, Nairobi: Konrad Adenauer Foundation.

Kwame, S. (2017), "Rethinking the History of African philosophy," in A. Afolayan and T. Falola (eds.), *The Palgrave handbook of African Philosophy*, 97–104, New York: Palgrave Macmillan.

Lamola, J. (2016), "On a Contextual South African Philosophy Curriculum: Towards an Option for the Excluded," *South African Journal of Philosophy*, 35 (4): 501–12.

Lavabre, M. C. (2009), "Historiography and Memory," in A. Tucker (ed.), *A Companion to the Philosophy of History and Historiography*, 362–70, New York: Blackwell Publishing.

Li-Hsiang, L. R. (2020), "A Revisionist History of Philosophy," *Journal of World Philosophies*, 5: 121–37.

Mafeje, A. (2000), "Africanity: A Combative Ontology," *CODESRIA Bulletin*, 1: 66–71.

Mall, R. A. (2014), "Intercultural Philosophy: A Conceptual Clarification," *Confluence: Journal of World Philosophies*, 1: 67–84.

Mamdani, M. (1998), "Is African Studies To Be Turned Into A New Home For Bantu Education At UCT?" Available at: http://www.hartford-hwp.com/archives/30/136.html. (Accessed March 22, 2016.)

Mamdani, M. (2016), "Between the Public Intellectual and the Scholar: Decolonisation and Some Post-independence Initiatives in African Higher Education," *Inter-Asia Cultural Studies*, 17 (1): 68–83.

Margolis, J. (1995), *Historied Thought, Constructed World: A Conceptual Primer for the Turn of the Millennium*. Berkeley: University of California Press.

Masaka, D. (2017), "Challenging Epistemicide through Transformation and Africanisation of the Philosophy Curriculum in Africa," *South African Journal of Philosophy*, 36 (4): 441–55.

Masolo, D. A. (1994), *African Philosophy in Search of Identity*, Indianapolis: Indiana University Press.

Masolo, D. A. (1997), "African Philosophy: A Historical Overview," in E. Deutsch and R. Bontekoe (eds.), *A Companion to World Philosophies*, 63–77, New York: Blackwell Publishers.

Masolo D. A. (2000), "From Myth to Reality: African Philosophy at Century-end," *Research in African Literatures*, 31 (1): 149–72.

Matolino, B. (2019), "Ethnophilosophy as a Dead Discourse: Are We Finished with the Ethnophilosophy Debate? A Multi-perspective Conversation," *Filosofia Theoretica: Journal of African Philosophy, Culture, and Religions*, 8 (2): 111–37.

Matolino, B. (2020), "Philosophers' Debt to Their Students: The South African Case," *Transformation in Higher Education*, 5 (0), a87: 1–9, https://doi.org/10.4102/the.v5i0.87

Metz, T. (2017), "The Assumptions of Cross-cultural Philosophy: What Makes It Possible to Learn from Other Traditions," *Journal of World Philosophies*, 2: 99–107

Metz, T. (2018), "What is the Essence of an Essence? Comparing Afro-relational and Western-Individualist Ontologies," *Synthesis Philosophica*, 65 (1): 209–24.

Mkandawire, T., ed. (2005), *African Intellectuals: Rethinking Politics, Language, Gender and Development*, London: Zed Books.

Monahan, M. (2019), "Editor's Introduction," *The Southern Journal of Philosophy*, 57: 5–15.

Monahan, M. (2019a), "Reflections on Decolonising Philosophy: Can There Be Universality Without Universalism?" *Journal of World Philosophies*, 4: 82–6.

More, P. (2004), "Philosophy in South Africa Under and After Apartheid," in K. Wiredu (ed.), *A Companion to African Philosophy*, 149–60, Oxford: Blackwell Publishing.

Mudimbe, V. Y. (1988), *The Invention of Africa: Gnosis, Philosophy and the Order of Knowledge*, Indianapolis: Indiana University Press.

Mukandi, B. (2019), "Beyond Hermes: Metaphysics in a New Key," *Utafiti: Journal of African Perspectives*, 14 (1): 152–68.

Mungwini, P. (2012), "Surveillance and Cultural Panopticism: Situating Foucault in African Modernities," *South African Journal of Philosophy*, 31 (2), 340–53.

Mungwini, P. (2015), "Dialogue as the Negation of Hegemony: An African Perspective," *South African Journal of Philosophy*, 34 (4): 395–407.

Mungwini, P. (2016), "The Question of Recentring Africa: Thoughts and Issues from the Global South," *South African Journal of Philosophy*, 35 (4): 523–36.

Mungwini, P. (2017), *Indigenous Shona Philosophy: Reconstructive insights*, Pretoria: AHP & Unisa Press.

Mungwini, P. (2017a), "African Know Thyself: Epistemic Injustice and the Quest for Liberative Knowledge," *International Journal of African Renaissance Studies: Multi-, Inter- and Transdiscipinarity*, 12 (2): 5–18.

Mungwini, P. (2017b), "Pan-Africanism and Epistemologies of the South," *Theoria: A Journal of Social & Political Theory*, 64 (153): 165–86.

Mungwini, P. (2018), "The Question of Epistemic Justice: Polemics, Contestations and Dialogue," *Phronimon*, 19: 1–13.

Mungwini, P. (2019), "The Critique of Ethnophilosophy in the Mapping and Trajectory of African Philosophy," *Filosofia Theoretica: Journal of African Philosophy, Culture and Religions*, 8 (3): 1–20.

Mungwini, P. (2019a), "The Quest for Epistemic Liberation: What Can Be Done to Be True to Both Philosophy and to Humanity?" *Journal of World Philosophies*, 4: 70–7.

Mungwini, P. (2020), "Struggles for Self-liberation in African Philosophy," *Phronimon*, 21: 1–12 https://doi.org/10.25159/2413–3086/7509

Mungwini, P. (2021), "Decolonisation Debates in Higher Education," in A. Ndofirepi and E. T. Gwaravanda (eds.), *African Higher Education in the 21st Century: Some Philosophical Dimensions*, 106–21, Leiden: Brill.

Ndlovu-Gatsheni, S. (2013), "Why Decoloniality in the 21st Century?" *The Thinker*, 48: 10–15.

Nkrumah, K. (1964), *Consciencism: Philosophy and Ideology for Decolonization and Development with Particular Reference to the African Revolution*, New York: Modern Reader Paperbacks.

Nkrumah, K. (1965), *Neo-colonialism: The Last Stage of Imperialism*, London: Thomas Nelson & Sons.

Nkrumah, K. (1967), "African Socialism Revisited," https://www.marxists.org/subject/africa/nkrumah/1967/african-socialism-revisited.htm. (Accessed March 9, 2021.)

Nyerere, J. K. (1968), *Freedom and Socialism*, Oxford: Oxford University Press.

Ochieng, O. (2010), "The African Intellectual: Hountondji and After," *Radical Philosophy*, 164: 25–37.

Oguejiofor, J. O. (2009), "Negritude as Hermeneutics: A Reinterpretation of Leopold Sedar Senghor's Philosophy," *American Catholic Philosophical Quarterly*, 83 (1): 79–94.

Oguejiofor, J. O. (2019), "African philosophy in South Africa: the model of Mogobe Ben Ramose," in H. Lauer and H. Yitah (eds.), *The Tenacity of Truthfulness: Philosophical Essays in Honour of Mogobe Bernard Ramose*, 101–30, Dar es Salaam: Mkuki Na Nyota.

Okere, T. (1983), *African Philosophy: A Historico-Hermeneutical Investigation of the Conditions of its Possibility*, Lanham, MD: University Press of America.

Okere, T. (2003), "Philosophy and Intercultural Dialogue," http://www. urbaniana.com/news2004/12_03_04.htm. (Accessed January 26, 2020.)

Okere, T. (2005), "Is There One Science, Western Science?" *Africa Development*, 30 (3): 20–34.

Okere, T. (2018), "The Self," *Plenary Session Paper* of the 24th World Congress of Philosophy, Beijing, 28–47.

Okolo, C. B. (2002), "Self As a Problem in African Philosophy," in P. H. Coetzee and A. P. J. Roux (eds.), *The African Philosophy Reader*, 209–18, Cape Town: Oxford University Press of South Africa.

Osuagwu, I. M. (1999), *African Historical Reconstruction. Vol. 1*, Owerri: Assumpta Press.

Outlaw, L. T., Jr. (1992), "African, African American, Africana Philosophy," *The Philosophical Forum*, 24 (1–3): 63–93.

Outlaw, L.T. Jr (1996), *On race and Philosophy*, New York: Routledge.

Outlaw, L. T., Jr. (2002), "African Philosophy: Deconstructive and Reconstructive Challenges," in P. H. Coetzee and A. P. J. Roux (eds.), *The African Philosophy Reader*, 162–85, Cape Town: Oxford University Press of South Africa.

Outlaw, L. T., Jr. (2004), "Africana Philosophy: Origins and Prospects," in K. Wiredu (ed.), *A Companion to African Philosophy*, 90–8, Oxford: Blackwell Publishing.

Outlaw, L. T., Jr. (2007), "Social Ordering and the Systematic Production of Ignorance," in S. Sullivan and N. Tuana (eds.), *Race and Epistemologies of Ignorance*, 197–211, Albany: State University of New York Press.

Outlaw, L T., Jr. (2017), "'Black' Philosophy, 'African' Philosophy, 'Africana' Philosophy: Transnational Deconstructive and Reconstructive Renovations in 'Philosophy'," in A. Afolayan and T. Falola, (eds.), *The Palgrave handbook of African Philosophy*, 245–67, New York: Palgrave Macmillan.

Park, K. J. P. (2013), *Africa, Asia, and the History of Philosophy: Racism in the Formation of the Philosophical Canon, 1780–1830*, Albany, NY: State University of New York.

Plant, B. (2017), "On the Domain of Metaphilosophy," *Metaphilosophy* 48 (1–2): 3–24.

Plantinga, A. (1984), "Advice to Christian Philosophers," *Faith and Philosophy: Journal of the Society of Christian Philosophers*, 1 (3): 253–71.

Popper, K. (1959), *The Logic of Scientific Discovery*, New York: Harper & Row Publishers.

Pratt, M. L. (2008), "In the Neocolony: Destiny, Destination, and the Traffic in Meaning," in B. Morana, E. Dussel, and C. A. Jauregui (eds.), *Coloniality at Large: Latin America and the Postcolonial Debate*, 459–75, Durham, NC: Duke University Press.

Ramose, M. B. (1999), *African Philosophy through Ubuntu*, Harare: Mond Books.

Ramose, M. B. (2000), "'African renaissance': A Northbound Gaze," *Politeia*, 19 (3): 47–61.

Ramose, M. B. (2001), "An African Perspective on Justice and Race," *Polylog* https://them.polylog.org/3/frm-en.htm. (Accessed May 26, 2021.)

Ramose, M. B. (2002), "I Conquer, Therefore I Am the Sovereign: Reflections Upon Sovereignty, Constitutionalism, and Democracy in Zimbabwe and South Africa," in P. H. Coetzee and A. P. J. Roux (eds.), *The African Philosophy Reader*, 543–89, Cape Town: Oxford University Press of South Africa.

Ramose, M. B. (2005), "Philosophy: A Particularist Interpretation with Universal Appeal," in J. O. Oguejiofor and G. I. Onah (eds.), *African Philosophy and the Hermeneutics of Culture: Essays in Honour of Theophilus Okere*, 145–60, Munster: LITT.

Ramose, M. B. (2013), "Introduction," in M. B. Ramose (ed.), *Hegel's Twilight: Liber Amicorum Discipulorumque Pro Heinz Kimmerle*, 7–9, Amsterdam: Rodopi.

Ramose, M. B, (2014), "Dying a Hundred Deaths: Socrates on Truth and Justice," *Phronimon*, 15 (1): 67–80.

Ramose, M. B. (2014a), "Ubuntu: Affirming a right and seeking remedies in South Africa," in L. Praeg and S. Magadla (eds.), *Ubuntu: Curating the Archive*, 121–36, Pietermaritzburg: UKZN Press.

Ramose, M. B. (2015), "On the Contested Meaning of 'Philosophy'," *South African Journal of Philosophy* 34 (4): 551–8.

Ramose, M. B. (2018), "Towards a Post-conquest South Africa: Beyond the Constitution of 1996," *South African Journal of Human Rights*, 34 (3): 326–41.

Ree, J. (2001), "The Translation of Philosophy," *New Literary History*, 2 (2): 223–57.

Ree, J. (2002), "Women Philosophers and the Canon," *British Journal for the History of Philosophy*, 10 (4): 641–52.

Rettova, A. (2016), "Editorial: African Philosophy as a Radical Critique," *Journal of African Cultural Studies*, 28 (2): 127–31.

Samkange, S. and Samkange T. M. (1980), *Hunhuism or Ubuntuism: A Zimbabwean Indigenous Political Philosophy*, Salisbury: Graham Publishing.

Santos, B. S., J. A. Nunes, and M. P. Meneses (2007), "Opening Up the Canon of Knowledge and Recognition of Difference," in B. S. Santos (ed.), *Another Knowledge is Possible*, xix–lxii, London: Verso.

Santos, B. S. (2014), *Epistemologies of the South: Justice against Epistemicide*, London: Paradigm Publishers.

Sarton, G. (1927), *Introduction to the History of Science: Volume 1, from Homer to Omar Khayyam*, Baltimore: The Williams and Wilkins Company.

Schacht, R. (1993), "On Philosophy's Canon, and its 'Nutzen und Nachteil'," *The Monist*, 76 (4): 421–35.

Serequeberhan, T. (1994), *The Hermeneutics of African Philosophy: Horizon and Discourse*, New York: Routledge.

Serequeberhan, T. (1997), "The Critique of Eurocentrism and the Practice of African Philosophy," in E. C. Eze (ed.), *Postcolonial African Philosophy: A Critical Reader*, 141–61, London: Blackwell Publishers.

Serequeberhan, T. (2009), "African Philosophy as the Practice of Resistance," *Journal of Philosophy: A Cross-Disciplinary Inquiry*, 4 (9): 44–52.

Serequeberhan, T. (2011), "African Philosophy: Prospects and Possibilities," in W. Edelglass and J. L. Garfield (eds.), *The Oxford Handbook of World Philosophy*, DOI: 10.1093/oxfordhb/9780195328998.003.0040

Serequeberhan, T. (2015), *Existence and Heritage: Hermeneutic Explorations in African and Continental Philosophy*, Albany, NY: State University of New York Press.

Serequeberhan T. (2019), "Africa, Modernity, Freedom," *Revista de Estudios Africanos*, Numero Cero:1–22, http://doi.org/10.15366/reauam2019.0.001

Shivji, I. G. (2014), "Utu, Usawa, Uhuru: Building Blocks of Nyerere's Political Philosophy," in L. Praeg, and S. Magadla (eds.), *Ubuntu: Curating the Archive*, 137–49, Pietermaritzburg: UKZN Press.

Smart, N. (1999), *World Philosophies*, London: Routledge.

Solomon, R.C. (1999), *The Joy of Philosophy*, Oxford: Oxford University Press.

Solomon, R. C. (2001), "'What Is Philosophy?' The Status of World Philosophy in the Profession', *Philosophy East and West*, 51 (1): 100–04.

Soyinka, W. (1976), *Myth, Literature and the African World*, London: Cambridge University Press.

Storm, W. (1993), "Bantoe-Filosofe vs Bantu Philosophy," *Quest: An International African Journal of Philosophy*, 7 (2): 67–75.

Strickland, L. (2018), "Western Philosophy Departments Must Open Their Minds," Metro https://www.mmu.ac.uk/news-and-events/news/story/?id=7283. (Accessed October 1, 2020.)

Strickland, L. (2019), "How Western Philosophy Became Racist," IAI News, https://iai.tv/articles/the-racism-of-the-western-philosophy-canon-auid-1200. (Accessed October 1, 2020.)

Taiwo, O, (2004), "Post-independence African Political Philosophy," in K. Wiredu (ed.), *A Companion to African Philosophy*, 243–59, Oxford: Blackwell Publishing.

Tempels, P. (1959), *Bantu Philosophy*, trans. Rev C. Colin, Paris: Presence Africaine.

Van Hensbroek, P. B. (2013), "Beyond Crossing Borders: Beyond Intercultural Philosophy," in M. B. Ramose (ed.), *Hegel's Twilight: Liber Amicorum Discipulorumque: Pro Heinz Kimmerle*, 31–41, Amsterdam: Rodopi.

Wallerstein, I. (1995), *Historical Capitalism with Capitalist Civilisation*, Verso: New York.

Wa Thiong'o, N. (1987), *Decolonising the Mind: the Politics of Language in African Literatures*, Harare: ZPH.

Wa Thiong'o, N. (2012), *Globalectics: Theory and the Politics of Knowing*, New York: Columbia University Press.

Wa Thiong'o, N. (2013), "Tongue and Pen: A Challenge to Philosophers from Africa', *Journal of African Cultural Studies*, 25 (2): 158–63.

Wimmer, F. M. (2007), "Cultural Centrisms and Intercultural Polylogues in Philosophy," *International Review of Information Ethics*, 7: 1–8.

Wimmer, F. M. et al., eds (2010), *Intercultural Philosophy: New Aspects and Methods*, Frankfurt: Peter Lang.

Wiredu, K. (1980), *Philosophy and an African Culture*, Cambridge: Cambridge University Press.

Wiredu, K. (1992), "The Ghanaian Tradition of Philosophy," in K. Wiredu, and K. Gyekye (eds.), *Person and Community: Ghanaian Philosophical Studies, 1*, 1–12, Washington DC: Council for Research in Values and Philosophy.

Wiredu, K. (1996), *Cultural Universals and Particulars*, Bloomington: Indiana University Press.

Wiredu, K. (1998), "Toward Decolonising African Philosophy and Religion," *African Studies Quarterly*, 1 (4): 17–46

Wiredu, K. (1998a), "Can Philosophy Be Intercultural? An African Viewpoint," *Diogenes*, 46 (4): 147–67.

Wiredu, K. (2004), "Introduction: African Philosophy in Our Time," in

K. Wiredu (ed.), *A Companion to African Philosophy*, 1–27, Oxford: Blackwell Publishing.

Wiredu, K. (2010), "African Religions from a Philosophical Point of View," in C. Taliafero, P. Draper, and P. L. Quinn (eds.), *A Companion to Philosophy of Religion*, 34–43, Oxford: Blackwell Publishing.

Wiredu, K. (2011), "Empiricalism: The Empirical Character of an African Philosophy," in H. Lauer, N. A. A. Amfo, and J. A. Anderson (eds.), *Identity meets Nationality: Voices from the Humanities*, 17–34, Legon: Sub-Saharan Publishers.

Yancy, G. (2013), "Performing Philosophical Dialogue As a Space for *Dwelling Near*," *Philosophia Africana*, 15 (2): 99–105.

Zeleza, P. T. (2002), "The Politics of Historical and Social Science Research in Africa," *Journal of Southern African Studies*, 28 (1): 9–23.

Zeleza, T. P. (2007), *The Study of Africa Vol.2: Global and Transnational Engagements*, Dakar: CODESRIA.

Zene, C. (2015), "World Philosophies in Dialogue: A Shared Wisdom?" *Confluence: Journal of World Philosophies*, 2: 11–32.

Index